Cow

Animal

Series editor: Jonathan Burt

Cow

Hannah Velten

REAKTION BOOKS

For my brother, Christian Velten

Published by
REAKTION BOOKS LTD
33 Great Sutton Street
London EC1V 0DX, UK
www.reaktionbooks.co.uk

First published 2007
Copyright © Hannah Velten 2007

Printed and bound in China

British Library Cataloguing in Publication Data
Velten, Hannah
   Cow. – (Animal)
   1. Cattle 2. Cattle – History 3. Animals and civilization
   4. Human-animal relationships
   I. Title
   636.2

ISBN-13: 978 1 86189 326 0
ISBN-10: 1 86189 326 4

Contents

Michael J Austin, *Right of Way*, 2005, oil on canvas. This is a fighting bull from Andalusia, southern Spain, painted 'at home' – a breeding ranch in the country.

Introduction: Reintroducing the Cow, Bull and Ox

In no animal is there to met with a greater variety of kinds;
and in none, a more humble and pliant disposition . . . a
source of inexhaustible wealth – the pride and boast of this
happy country.
Thomas Bewick, *A General History of Quadrupeds* (1790)

There are over 1.37 billion cattle in the world.[1] How many have you met? Chances are if you live in the West, not many, or none. You can imagine being close to a cow: experiencing their weighty bulk near you, feeling their hot, grassy breath on your face, touching their cool, slimy muzzle or experiencing their curling, sandpaper-like tongue licking your skin. Our ancestors would have known this close contact with cattle, living and working with them, relying on them almost exclusively for food and labour, and even sharing their diseases.

This unique relationship between humans and cattle has shaped millennia of global history and culture – both in religious and secular life. In fact, as one commentator states, 'No other event in early history was of such comparably far reaching significance for the development of human culture as the domestication of oxen.'[2]

From their limited global beginnings in the Near East, the Indus Valley and Africa, the 'man-made' domestic cow followed in the wake of human movement; becoming the symbol of a civilized life. Cattle were revered, loved, exalted and romanticized.

Today, cattle are on virtually every continent in the world and the word 'cow' is recognized in 539 different languages and dialects.[3] Yet, in the West, most cows are hidden away on farms where only a few lucky people continue to relate with them.

We do have a cattle culture of sorts in the modern Western world, but it is generally not a happy lot for the cow. Cattle cultures are now big business: dictated by the consumers, fast-food outlets and supermarkets, processors, abattoirs, transporters, auctioneers, commodity traders, vets and scientists – there are few romantic associations attached to modern cattle production, except the sight of cattle grazing in the fields.

But what does this mean for cows, and our relationship with them? Our huge, urban societies demand a steady supply of lean meat, wholesome milk and leather, of a uniform quality at a reasonable price. To meet these demands, the cow has been turned into an object – one that is bred, reared and grown to specification, as cheaply as possible, which means essentially that economies of scale dictate the means of production.

Although cattle have largely escaped the excesses of intensive production compared with pigs and poultry, there are now far fewer people looking after more cows than ever before: this is as true of cattle in automated beef-lots as of those being raised on cattle stations in Latin America and Australia.

If there are fewer people looking after cattle, is it obvious that the majority of beef- and veal-eaters, milk-drinkers and leather-wearers have not the slightest link with cattle. As a consequence, most cattle production, transportation and slaughter goes on behind 'closed doors', and it is only through investigative journalism, animal rights campaigners, environmentalists and the mass media that our current cultural views and opinions of cattle are formed. As a result, people today are generally ignorant of cattle: for example, few realize that the cow has to have a calf before she will give milk; she does not produce milk naturally for humans. In a media-informed age, you may see the cow as a staggering, BSE-infected 'mad cow', an exploited 'poor cow', an environment-polluting 'hoofed locust'[4] or an esteemed 'sacred cow'?

Apart from the last-named, the images we are fed of cattle are essentially negative. Hopefully, this potted cultural history of cattle will reintroduce you to the bull, cow, ox and calf as your ancestors would have viewed them: in a positive light, as fearsome adversaries, mythical beings, as mobile wealth and respected animal companions.

John Kenny *Lady in White*, 2005, giclée print on Hahnemuhle Rag paper. Among the sacred cows of Gujarat, India.

These terms are used throughout the book:

> *bull* entire male
> *cow* female who has produced a calf
> *heifer* young female who is yet to calve
> *ox* castrated male used as a source of power
> *steer* castrated male used for beef production

1 Wild Ox to Domesticates

Domestic or 'true' cattle belong to the order *Artiodactyla* (mammals with an even numbers of toes on each foot), and along with sheep, goats and antelope, cattle belong to the family of horned, ruminant herbivores called *bovidae* (bovines). Within this family, cattle belong to the sub-family *bovinae* and the genus *Bos*.

Domestic cattle throughout the world are all descended from a single wild species, *Bos primigenius*, the recently extinct wild ox or 'aurochs' (spelled the same in the singular and plural). However, the earliest representative of the genus *Bos* was named *Leptobos*, which appeared in the early Pleistocene (*c.* 2 million years ago) in Asia. These antelope-like mammals were rather slim, stood about two metres high and were three metres long. The *Leptobos* evolved into *Bos primigenius* during the late Pleistocene and, as the global grass area expanded, the aurochs migrated into the Middle East and north-east Africa, finally reaching Europe about 250,000 years ago.[1]

At their peak, aurochs were widespread over the temperate zones of the northern hemisphere, but never reached Ireland, central and northern Scandinavia or North America. To cope with the differing environments over this huge area, they evolved into three different strains: the Indian/Asian type, *Bos primigenius namadicus*; the Near East and European type, *Bos*

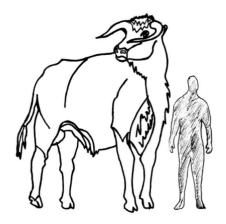

The aurochs' earliest ancestors were rather slim and antelope-like, but they were nearly two metres high at the shoulder.

primigenius primigenius; and the African type, *Bos primigenius africanus* (*opisthonomus*).[2]

Their world was much wetter and therefore greener than today's. Aurochs chose to live in river valleys and marshy forests and, like their domestic descendents, they were true herbivores rather than just grazers. Their diet consisted of grass and herbs, tree foliage and bark in the spring and summer, acorns in the autumn and dry leaves in the winter. To digest this fibrous diet, the bovine family's stomach is divided into four distinct compartments: the rumen, the reticulum, the omasum and abomasum. This multi-chambered stomach allows them to eat plant matter that is too coarse for most mammals, including humans, to eat.

Symbiosis w/ bacteria to digest cellulose

The fibre is first fermented and digested in the rumen. This structure constantly churns the food with rhythmic contractions two to four times a minute, and with the help of rumen micro-organisms and bacteria the fibre is broken down. When cattle are resting, they voluntarily regurgitate some of the rumen content, chew a while, and then swallow it again, where it passes on to the reticulum. This ongoing process of second chewing is called rumination, or 'chewing the cud', and may occur for eight hours out of twenty-four in cattle.[3]

FEARSOME QUARRY

The first evidence of human contact with aurochs can be seen in European cave paintings. After horses and bison, aurochs were the third most represented animal during the Upper Palaeolithic period.[4] However, in the Lascaux caves in south-west France (decorated in about 17,000 BC), aurochs take centre stage, being depicted 52 times. There are the majestic figures in the Rotunda (The Hall of the Bulls), the cows and bull in the Axial Gallery and the Great Black Cow in the Nave.

'The Hall of the Bulls' in the Lascaux caves, France, where images of aurochs dominate the walls and ceilings.

It is still unclear what these images of aurochs represent, but because the paintings are placed in the central areas of the caves, rather than being hidden away, the aurochs was obviously an important animal. These depictions could represent a record of hunting trophies, or serve a religious or social function, possibly totems of a tribal clan or as symbols of supernatural power. Whatever their purpose, the rock art gives us an idea of what the Palaeolithic aurochs of Europe looked like.

Although they were large, squarely built animals, there was a fair size difference between the sexes, which originally misled archaeologists and zoologists to wrongly conclude there was a dwarf-aurochs.[5] The cows were smaller and lighter, had slenderer heads and shorter horns than the bulls. The bulls stood just under two metres in height and weighed about 1.3 tonnes. There seems to have been a range of coat colours among bulls of differing regions. Northern European bulls were mostly black-brown in colour, with a narrow lighter stripe along their backs, whereas the southern European bulls were brown or grey-brown. The cows and calves of all regions were reddish-brown.

Aurochs' horns grew up to two metres long, pointing forwards and curving inwards. The weight of the horns must have been immense, but this did not stop the aurochs from being agile. It was a feared quarry: an Anglo-Saxon runic verse from the ninth century, found in north Germany, states

The aurochs is fearless and large-horned,
a fierce animal – it fights with its horns –
the famous marsh walker; it is a brave animal.[6]

The hunting of the aurochs is well documented, but mainly in terms of the challenge that they presented. Even if the hunters went for the weak or young animals in a herd, they

An aurochs depicted by Heberstain, 1549 – but he does not look nearly agile enough!

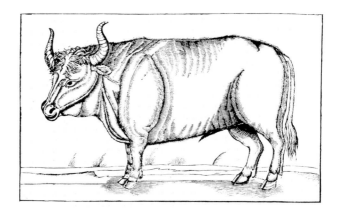

would have had the king bull to contend with, who would protect his cows and calves.

So why were they hunted? The huge carcass of an aurochs would provide enough rewards. Aside from meat, the Mesolithic hunters of Europe (8000–3000 BC) found many other uses for the carcasses: they used the bones (tools and jewellery), hides (clothing), horns (for carrying/storing liquid and ritual decorations), sinews (thread) and fat (oils).[7]

But these resources may have been of secondary importance to the cultural benefits of hunting down and slaying an aurochs, purely because of the risks it held. As early civilizations developed, it could have been a test of manhood or an initiation rite for young men, with the horns of the aurochs being kept as trophies and as ancestral reminders.[8] Aurochs hunting also became somewhat of a hobby, or duty, of the aristocracy. The Assyrian monarch Tiglath-Pileser I (1115–1076 BC) used the kudos of aurochs hunting to illustrate his aggression, cruelty and divine right. A description of the event reads:

The gods Hercules and Nergal gave their valiant servants and their arrows as a glory to support my empire. Under the auspices of Hercules, my guardian deity, four wild bulls, strong and fierce, in the desert, in the country of Mitan, and in the city Arazik, belonging to the country of the Khatte, with my long arrows tipped with iron, and with heavy blows I took their lives. Their skins and their horns I brought to my city of Ashur.[9]

It seems that large numbers of aurochs were hunted, as seen in a description of possibly the last aurochs hunt in Egypt by Pharaoh Amenhotep III (1417–1379 BC) and his army.[10] A gruesome total of ninety-six bulls were reportedly killed over the course of two hunts, when a group of bulls, spotted in the desert, were driven into an enclosure containing a ditch. Once trapped in the ditch, they were slaughtered.[11]

Long after the aurochs became extinct in Egypt,[12] they could still be found in the Hercynian Forest in Germany, where they

Pharaoh Rameses III and his armies hunting the aurochs along the banks of the Nile: stone relief at Medinet Habu (Rameses III mortuary temple), c. 1100 BC.

were hunted as the prize kill. Julius Caesar (100–44 BC) encountered the *urus* – Latin for aurochs – in 53 BC, giving this description in his *De Bello Gallico* (*The Gallic War*):

> They are slightly smaller than elephants, and in appearance, colour, and shape they resemble bulls. They are extremely fierce and swift-footed, and attack people and animals on sight. The Germans carefully trap them in pits, and then slaughter them. Such tasks make the young German men tough, and this type of hunting gives them training. Those who kill the most wild oxen display the horns in public as a proof, which wins them considerable acclaim. The oxen cannot grow accustomed to people, or become tame, even if they are caught when young. The size, appearance, and shape of their horns are very different from the horns of our own cattle. These horns are much prized: the Germans give them a rim of silver and use them as drinking-vessels at magnificent feasts.[13]

While aurochs' horns were the main hunting trophies, Polish kings were said to favour the aurochs' heart bones (there are two small bones in the bovine heart) and their curly, shaggy forehead skin as trophies. The skin was cut loose in a circle

Thomas Bewick, 'Wild Cattle', vignettes from *History of Quadrupeds* (1790): The same bull features in 'The Chillingham Bull', which he sketched in 1789. Bewick tells of the difficulty he had getting close enough to the wild cattle to draw them properly, without being chased.

while the aurochs was still alive and then torn off. When ripped into shreds and worn as a belt, this skin was said to help pregnant women give birth with ease.[14]

Poland had, and still has, a special connection with the aurochs: it was their final resting place. By the fifteenth century, due to loss of habitat, grazing competition from their domesticated descendents, disease and hunting, aurochs were found only in the Jaktorowski Royal Forest in Mazowsze in Central Poland. It was here that they enjoyed legal protection under the Crown. Only officially appointed hunters were allowed to kill dangerous bulls, or those which mated with domestic cattle (the offspring were never viable), and the local population,

'Heck cattle' or 'reconstituted aurochs', seen here at the Lejre Experimental Centre, Denmark, 2006: the open-air museum has recreated ancient villages and re-enacts ancient lifestyles.

rather than paying taxes, acted as gamekeepers and fed the aurochs hay over the winter. But, finally, the last aurochs cow died a natural death in 1627.

There have been efforts to recreate the aurochs since its demise. At the end of the 1920s, the 'Aurochs makers' brothers Heinz and Lutz Heck tried, in the zoos of Munich and Berlin respectively, to back-breed primitive forms of domestic breeds of cattle with aurochs-like qualities, such as English Park Cattle and Scottish Highland. The results of the two breeding experiments – the 'reconstituted' aurochs – were largely similar, but today only animals from the Munich-type survive, mainly in zoos and reserves. While they appear to look like true aurochs (colour and horns) and have a ferocious temper, they never reached the size of aurochs or achieved the size differences between cow and bull.

The aurochs gained the dubious honour of being the first documented case of extinction (the second being the dodo).[15] And, although the drier climate reduced their habitat, it was humans who initiated their eventual downfall through hunting (with pitfalls, nets, spears and arrows) and woodland clearance for cattle pasture – a sad end to a species which gave human civilizations arguably their most important domestic animals: cattle.

In about 7,000 BC, the first humans decided that they should begin a closer relationship with the ferocious aurochs. But why they should attempt to tame the beasts when they already had domestic sheep and goats, providing them with meat, milk and skins, is open to debate. Even archaeologists could not believe that domestic cattle derived from the dangerous aurochs. In 1846 Professor Richard Owen found remains of small, short-horned cattle in peat bogs in Ireland, which he labelled *Bos longifrons*, thinking that he had found the true ancestor of the domestic cow.[16]

Theories for cattle domestication are varied, but one from Eduard Hahn (published 1896, 1909) emphasizes the religious/spiritual associations that early civilizations made with the aurochs (see chapter Two). The moon with its regularly changing phases was a fertility symbol, and the crescent-shaped horns of the aurochs became associated with lunar goddesses. Regular animal sacrifices were used to placate the goddesses in order to maintain the fertility of their crops and animals, so a regular supply of less aggressive and more docile aurochs would have been welcomed.

Other theorists, notably F. E. Zeuner (1963), envisage cattle domestication as a by-product of human's ongoing battle to save their crops from the 'hoofed crop-robbers' (aurochs):

> While struggling to keep the large animals out of his fields, man would no doubt have captured and kept in his settlements the calves – a habit well known from modern

primitive tribes . . . Having tied these animals up in his camp, however, man would not have bothered much about their feeding and, in course of time and on a near-starvation diet, a smaller, more passive generation would grow up within the precincts of human settlements. Thus the large ruminants came as crop-robbers and ended up as domesticated beasts.[17]

Having inadvertently tamed a few aurochs, it would have been fairly easy to increase the herd either by letting nature take its course, by luring wild aurochs near to the settlement (especially with salt licks), or by capturing them and introducing them to the tamed animals. To illustrate how the latter method may have worked, in 1834 Charles Darwin recorded a hunting expedition with the *gauchos* (Argentine 'cowboys') to capture feral cattle while visiting East Falkland Island:

> When hunting, the party endeavours to get as close as possible to the herd without being discovered. Each man carries four or five pair of the bolas [a missile consisting of a number of balls connected by strong cord]; these he throws one after the other at as many cattle, which, when once entangled, are left for some days till they become a little exhausted by hunger and struggling. They are then let free and driven towards a small herd of tame animals, which have been brought to the spot on purpose. From their previous treatment, being too much terrified to leave the herd, they are easily driven, if their strength last out, to the settlement.[18]

Cattle are gregarious creatures and, as such, will always live in herds and become exceedingly anxious when separated from their group. The English naturalist Gilbert White (1720–93), in his observations of the wildlife around his Selborne home in Hampshire, remarked of cattle:

> There is a wonderful spirit of sociality in the brute creation, independent of sexual attachment . . . Oxen and cows will not fatten by themselves; but will neglect the finest pasture that is not recommended by society.[19]

This quality would have made caught aurochs fairly easy to bunch together and restrain. And bovines have a well-defined hierarchy of dominance, which would mean that once a 'leader' was caught, the rest would follow.

To make handling these aurochs a safer occupation, it was also possible that their horns were pared down (a painful operation, as bovine horn contains nerve endings) and the males castrated. The ancient Egyptian fable of 'The Lion in Search of Man'[20] also mentions other cruel methods which man used to subdue cattle, including piercing their noses and threading rope through it, and then passing the rope over the top of another cow's head and then through their noses; so a line of cattle could be kept together.

CATTLE AS WEALTH

Possibly without even realizing the significance of what they were doing, it seems that humans domesticated the aurochs in three different areas in the Neolithic era between 6000–4000 BC: in the Fertile Crescent in the Near East, the Indus Valley (now Pakistan) and the south-eastern Sahara in Africa. Although each domestication centre had their own local strain of aurochs, domesticated cattle developed into two distinct types:

A magisterial Zebu bull adorns this clay impression of a carved seal. The stone seal would have been used to stamp clay tablets to indicate administrative dealings, or used to seal doors or containers, c. 2000 BC from the ancient Indus city of Mohenjo-daro.

the humpless (taurine) cattle (*Bos taurus*) developed in the Near East and Africa, while India produced the humped (zebu) cattle (*Bos indicus*).

It is no exaggeration to say that *Bos indicus* and *Bos taurus* played an enormous role in shaping civilization: mainly through the innovation of milking and the cultivation of land using the plough (see chapter Four). Previously nomadic peoples could begin to cultivate marginal soils, become sedentary and build villages and towns. As the populations in these towns grew, the domestic cow and oxen became a form of mobile wealth, which caused the early stratification of society.

The Roman scholar Varro Reatinus (116–27 BC) explained: *Omnis pecuniae pecus fundamentum* ('for cattle are the origin of all money' – the Latin word for wealth, *pecunia*, comes from the word for cattle, *pecus*).[21] The term 'cattle' is derived from the Middle English and Old Northern French *catel*, the late Latin *captale* and the Latin *capitale*, meaning 'capital' in the sense of chattel or chief property.

There were several methods developed to record cattle ownership. In Mesopotamia in the Near East, the Sumerian civilization was the first to develop a written symbol to denote cattle – the 'ox' sign. This stylized form of a cow's head was imprinted on damp clay tablets using a stylus, and dates from about 3100 BC. The tablets would have been used to record head numbers, and possibly to record bartering transactions. Similarly, in Ancient Egypt, the ideogram of 'cattle' was determined by a horned cow and was used to record the number of cattle owned by wealthy Egyptians and the temples, particularly during the bi-annual cattle count for taxation purposes. It was the numbers of cattle which was important, irrespective of the condition or the fatness of the individual animals.

Cattle were expensive to buy and also to maintain, so wealthy owners started to hire out their oxen and cows to those who could never afford to keep their own. This borrowing evidently caused friction. Law codes drawn up by King Hammurabi of Babylon in about 1750 BC show that out of 282 tersely written laws, 29 of the decipherable entries concern crimes against oxen and set out rules governing hiring payments and veterinary bills. For example:

248. If any one hire an ox, and break off a horn, or cut off its tail, or hurt its muzzle, he shall pay one-fourth of its value in money [to the owner].

251. If an ox be a goring ox, and it shown that he is a gorer, and he do not bind his horns, or fasten the ox up, and the ox gore a free-born man and kill him, the owner shall pay one-half a mina in money.

224. If a veterinary surgeon perform a serious operation on an ass or an ox, and cure it, the owner shall pay the surgeon one-sixth of a shekel as a fee.

225. If he perform a serious operation on an ass or ox, and kill it, he shall pay the owner one-fourth of its value.[22]

Apart from hiring out their cattle, owners also increased their wealth by trading animals with countries overseas – this was how zebu and taurine cattle spread from India and the Near East, respectively, from the third millennium BC. Zebu cattle had evolved to tolerate higher temperatures, more humid environments and to be more resistant to tropical diseases and insects than taurine cattle. For these reasons, zebus were traded outside India, probably most significantly to East Africa (via Arabia) where they were crossed with the local taurine breeds to produce more vigorous hybrid cattle.[23] Similarly, Australia and Latin America have most recently come to depend on the zebu genes to produce more drought and insect resistant breeds.

Meanwhile, taurine cattle also spread from the Near East via trade with the Indus Valley, and later via Greece, where they then followed Neolithic human migration on two paths: one by sea route into the western Mediterranean/Europe and another by land route into north-western Europe.

Wherever cattle landed, they helped to shape society and became valuable possessions. Pliny the Elder reported in *The Natural History* (c. AD 77) that oxen were 'our especial companion' and that they were considered by his Roman ancestors to

be of such value, that there was once an instance of a man being tried for killing an ox before the end of its working life. He had killed the beast in order to 'humour an impudent concubine of his, who said that she had never tasted tripe; and he was driven into exile, as though he had killed one of his own peasants'.[24]

Cattle also played a central role in Ireland after taurine breeds, which had arrived in England from the European mainland, were shipped over in about 3430 BC.[25] From early literary sources it appears that early Irish units of currency were based on the value of a cow: a *séd* was the value of one dairy (milch) cow and three *séd* made a *cumal* (female slave), being the value of three cows.[26]

CATTLE FOR SURVIVAL

Not only were cattle of economic importance, but they also meant survival for most European communities up until the mid-eighteenth century. When their cattle died, peoples' source of power and food also vanished (see chapter Four for the disastrous effects caused by loss of cattle on African pastoralists). This meant that great care was taken to protect the animals from plague (known as murrain or rinderpest), infertility and milk loss. But rather than relying on vaccinations and technology as we mainly do today, the Europeans practised rituals which they believed to ward off cattle diseases, and keep away the witches who stole milk from their cows.

According to the anthropologist James Frazer, the Celtic ritual fires at Easter, Beltane (May Day) and Midsummer's Eve played a major role in the purification of the cows.[27] To purify the cows after winter, and to bring luck for the coming year, the cows were either driven round the fires, driven through the fire's ashes or had the ashes mixed into their drinking water. It was as though the cattle plague was an evil force that could be kept at bay by a barrier of fire between it and the herds, and that witches were burnt or scared off by the heat of the fire.

If plague did strike then prayers were said, begging the Lord to put an end to the ordeal; or cow-leeches were employed. These people were the earliest known cattle 'veterinarians' in England, before the rise of rational medicine. Their methods were somewhat suspect, and relied on blood-letting and a range of herbal remedies to treat illness. One method for treating plague, described in 1648, was to dissolve a handful of hen's dung into a quart of old urine (presumably cows') and give it to all cattle to drink, whether they were sick, or in danger of becoming sick.[28]

However, diseases were not just passed between cattle; owning cattle could also prove fatal to the owners. As the cow and humans became more intimately connected (living and often sleeping in close proximity), greater was the chance of transferring infections and disease through faeces, urine, breath, sores and blood. American evolutionary biologist and author Jared Diamond has termed the diseases as 'deadly gifts' from cattle to mankind: tuberculosis, rinderpest (measles) and cowpox (smallpox).[29] These 'gifts' were passed on to the New World

The Cow-Pock _ or _ the Wonderful Effects of the New Inoculation! _ vide. the Publications of ŷ Anti Vaccine Society.

when European explorers arrived, bringing their cattle-derived diseases with them. For example, Christopher Columbus's second voyage to the West Indies (1493–6) took on board an unknown number of domesticated long-horned Spanish cattle, which he aimed to introduce to the island of Hispaniola (now the Dominican Republic) as part of his drive to found a mining-agricultural colony; a mini-Spanish civilization. Having never been exposed to cattle or their diseases, the indigenous peoples soon succumbed to the germs.[30]

'The Cow-Pock': caricature by James Gillray in 1802 showing Dr Edward Jenner inoculating patients at the Smallpox and Inoculation Hospital at St Pancras, London, with the frightening vision of cows emerging from human body parts. The word 'vaccination' comes from the Latin *vacca*, meaning 'cow'.

OTHER USES FOR CATTLE

Imports of more Spanish and Portuguese cattle continued intermittently into the Americas until the large imports of English

'Plowing on the Prairies . . .': ploughing oxen are the symbol of settled and civilized life. A wood-engraving (after a sketch by Theodore R. Davis) from *Harper's Weekly*, 9 May 1868.

PLOWING ON THE PRAIRIES BEYOND THE MISSISSIPPI.—[SKETCHED BY THEODORE R. DAVIS.]

cattle which came with the founders of the Jamestown colony in Virginia in 1611. These cattle were not only exported to provide milk, labour and meat for the settlers, but also came as symbols of English civilized life: it was thought that they could help build the English Empire.[31] In 1656 the House of Burgesses ruled that to give a cow to the Indians 'will be a step to civilizing them and to making them Christians'.[32] To gain their cow, the Indians had to present eight wolves' heads to the county officials and, in return, this cow could be used to cultivate their land; thus turning the Indians into settled, working farmers, rather than disordered, idle and chaotic hunters.

This may seem like a tall order for cattle (to 'civilize' the Indians), but, since they were first domesticated, humans have called upon cattle to act as mediators to miracles. Not only did the Shang dynasty of ancient China use the ox as a sacrificial animal, but its bones were also employed in divination ceremonies as 'oracle bones'. Questions about the future were written on ox scapulae, then the bones were heated with a brand until they cracked. These resulting cracks, which were 'supplied' by the royal ancestors, were the answers to the questions.

Humans have also employed cattle, dead or alive, for other unusual purposes (some less savoury than others). The Arabians used cattle flesh to help collect inaccessible cinnamon sticks, which were bought into Arabia by large birds. These birds used the sticks to line their mud nests, which they built on mountain precipices. Herodotus describes the method employed to collect the sticks in *The Histories* (440 BC):

> [The Arabians] cut up the bodies of dead oxen . . . into very large joints, which they carry to the spot in question and leave on the ground near the nests. They retire to a

The Roman marble *Farnese Bull* represents the Greek myth of Dirce, who was tied to a wild bull by the sons of Antiope to punish her for the ill-treatment inflicted on their mother, 1st century BC.

safe distance and the birds fly down and carry off the joints of meat to their nests, which, not being strong enough to bear the weight, break and fall to the ground. Then the men come along and pick up the cinnamon, which is subsequently exported to other countries.[33]

Herodotus also describes the execution method used by the nomadic Scythians to kill their 'lying' prophets or soothsayers, when their predictions or declarations were proved 'wrong':

> a cart is filled with sticks and harnessed to oxen; the guilty men, gagged and bound hand and foot, are thrust down amongst the sticks, which are then set alight, and the oxen scared off at a run. Often the oxen are burnt to death together with the soothsayers; often, too, the pole of the cart is burnt through enough to allow them to escape with a scorching.[34]

Similar fates were suffered by Christians who refused to make sacrifices to the bull-gods of pagan Europe, such as Sernin (Saturninus), the first bishop of Toulouse, who was reportedly tied to a bull that dragged him along, breaking his skull in two.

2 Bull-Gods, Bull-Kings

Wherever aurochs were indigenous, early civilizations regarded the bulls especially with awe and fear. These bulls were, for them, the supreme example of masculine strength and ferocity in nature, the epitome of fertility and virility. What better animal than the bull to associate with the gods who created your world, controlled the weather and dictated your well-being? It also followed that kings, whose power and authority were derived from the gods, were associated with the bull.

Bull-gods in all their fiery and thunderous glory were found in all early agrarian civilizations, where they were credited with providing the life-giving element of rain. They were storm gods who fertilized the soils, providing the crops that kept the agrarian/pastoral peoples alive. Bulls also became associated with gods of the sun and moon, the heavenly bodies upon which people relied for plant growth.

SYMBOL OF FERTILITY AND VIRILITY

In Mesopotamia, the Sumerian supreme deity was the bull-god Enlil, the god of the storm and of fertility. In legend it was Enlil and Ninlil, the cow or Mother goddess, whose marital union caused the rivers of the Tigris and Euphrates to rise and flood the land, giving fertility to the soil. Enlil was praised as the

Gilgamesh (*left*) and Enkidu (*right*) fighting the Bull of Heaven and another beast; cylinder-seal impression, c. 2340–2150 BC.

'Overpowering Ox' and was the father of Nannar, the moon-god who was also depicted as a bull, with particular emphasis on his horns. The association of the crescent-shaped horns of the bull and the waxing and waning of the moon was a powerful symbol of regeneration and rebirth. Sumerian kings such as Sargon wore horned headdresses and shared with Enlil the title of 'Wild Bull'. The people believed their kings derived their strength, power and authority from this supreme god, and many carvings and statues of bulls were humanized, by having them wear a kingly beard.

In *The Epic of Gilgamesh*, the legend of the historical Sumerian king of Uruk, Gilgamesh is described as 'Wild bull of Lugalbanda, Gilgamesh, the perfect in strength, / suckling of the august Wild Cow, the goddess Ninsun!'[1] But rather than being a king who protected and guided his people, he is tyrannical. He works his people hard with the building of the city, and he is sexually promiscuous, so that neither the wife of a noble, a mother's daughter nor the warrior's bride is safe from him.

His downfall begins when he angers the love goddess Ishtar by refusing her advances. She demands that her father Anu sends down to earth 'The Bull of Heaven' to kill Gilgamesh. The ferocious, divine bull arrives on earth and with his first snort opens a chasm in the ground, which kills one hundred men. The great

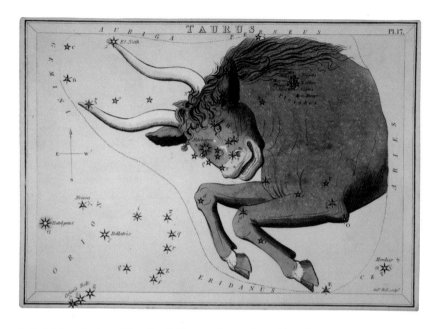

bull slobbers foul-smelling drool all over Gilgamesh, and brushes his companion Enkidu's face with its dirty tail. But the two heroes work together: while Enkidu holds the bull by the tail, Gilgamesh kills it with his sword.

Although they have triumphed over a mighty adversary, the gods punish them for slaying the sacred bull. Enkidu dies a lingering death and the distraught Gilgamesh realizes that he too is mortal. The spring of his youth, as a young bull, is over.

Such was the influence of the bull over the lives of the ancient inhabitants of Mesopotamia that they named the fertile spring in their calendar *Gut-sidi*, or the 'directing bull', and they were the first to identify and name the constellation of Taurus the Bull, as we know it now. They named it *Gut-anna* ('The Bull of Heaven' or 'The Bull's Jaw').

The constellation 'Taurus', from Jehoshaphat Aspin, *A Familiar Treatise on Astronomy . . .* (1825).

33

Over time, every major culture adapted the Taurus constellation to represent their specific myths and gods. The title of 'Bull' was translated into, or adapted to Greek (Tauros), Latin (Taurus), Sanskrit (Vrishaba), Persian (Gav) and Arabic (Thaur).[2]

Taurus later becomes a Western zodiac sign for the dates 21 April to 22 May. People born under this sign are said to be practical, reliable, patient, persistent, industrious, strong willed, sensuous, affectionate, warm hearted and trustworthy. On the downside, apparently they are also lazy, possessive, self-indulgent, dull, inflexible, unoriginal, unimaginative, greedy, stubborn and resentful.

EGYPT

Like the Sumerians, the Egyptian kings were also associated with the mighty wild bull, as seen in a number of Egyptian palettes made before 3050 BC. At this time, Egypt was a battleground for power struggles to control the small clusters of villages in Upper Egypt. The all-conquering supreme ruler is depicted as a bull triumphing over his human foes.[3]

But, while the rest of early civilizations were indiscriminately worshipping bulls, it was the Egyptians who believed that certain sacred bulls were the earthly embodiments of actual gods. The Mnevis bull was connected with the sun-god Ra in Heliopolis, and the Buchis bull was related to the war-god Montu at Armant.

However, probably the best-known sacred animal in Egypt was Apis, whose cult was established before 3000 BC. This bull was believed to embody the creator and fertility god Ptah, who was responsible for the periodic floods of the Nile which gave life to crops and to the Egyptian people.

When Apis died or was ritually sacrificed, an urgent search over the whole of Egypt took place to find a bull with the distinct

A fragment of
'The Bull Palette',
showing the
Egyptian bull-king
goring a foreign
adversary, c. 3120
BC.

markings of Ptah. In his *Histories*, Herodotus describes those markings, and how the bull was believed to have be created by Ptah, appearing as a celestial light:

> Now this Apis is a calf born of a cow who after this is not permitted to conceive any other offspring; and the Egyptians say that a flash of light comes down from heaven upon this cow, and of this she produces Apis. This calf which is called Apis is black and has the following signs, namely a white square upon the forehead, and on the back the likeness of an eagle, and in the tail the hairs are double, and on the tongue there is a mark like a beetle.[4]

Apis lived in sumptuous comfort, with the best food and a harem of cows, in a temple built exclusively for him, which stood opposite to the temple dedicated to Ptah. He was kept mainly in solitude, but took part in rituals and at a fixed hour every day he was let loose in the temple courtyard. Huge crowds of devoted followers, or indeed curious travellers, would gather to watch his antics and each of his movements was interpreted as foretelling the future. Pliny the Elder relates that when the Roman general Germanicus was murdered, it was remembered that just before his death the Apis bull had refused to eat from his hand.

Either Apis died naturally or, according to Plutarch, he was drowned in a holy spring if he reached the aged of twenty-five. This was so that his powers were never tempered by the weakness and frailty of old age. Passages from the 'Cannibal Hymn' of the Pyramid Texts indicate that the king would eat the flesh of the dead Apis to renew himself with the god Ptah's strength, power, and virility.

On his death, the body of Apis was mummified, enclosed in an immense sarcophagus of sandstone or pink granite, and buried in vast subterranean chambers at Saqqarah, after a splendid funeral service. It was believed that the bull-god's soul joined with that of Osiris, god of the underworld, to created Serapis, a fusion fertility god whose cult was adopted by the Greeks, and later the Romans.

Another bull taking part in Egyptian fertility rituals was the white bull of Min, the god of sex and fertility. The bull took part in the coronation rites of the pharaohs in the New Kingdom to ensure their sexual vigour and, hopefully, the birth of a male heir. The white bull was also honoured at harvest festivals, where he would be offered the first sheaves of wheat to ensure a plentiful harvest, and he presided over the hoeing festival to aid the fruitfulness of the earth.

It is likely that the Indus civilization also venerated the bull as a symbol of fertility, possibly serving as a consort to the Mother Goddess. But, the best accounts of bull worship come from the *Rig-Veda*, a collection of hymns written by the conquering Aryans from Indo-Europe, who brought their fertility bull-gods to India in the second millennium BC. The Aryans were pastoralists; descendents of the nomadic Eurasian steppes people who herded vast numbers of cattle, which they regarded as their wealth.

In Sanskrit, the language of the *Rig-Veda*, the words for 'bull' and for 'rain' are both derived from the same root word meaning 'to water' and 'to impregnate'.[5] Indra is the supreme bull-god of the thunderstorm, who vanquishes the demons of drought and darkness by making

> . . . his ally the thunder, and with its light milked cows
> from out the darkness.
> The waters flowed according to their nature.[6]

Like the generative storm, his temper is ferocious, and his strength legendary:

> Swift, rapidly striking, like a bull who sharpens his horns,
> terrific, stirring up the people,
> With eyes that close not, bellowing, Sole Hero, Indra,
> subdued at once a hundred armies.[7]

Almost three thousand years on, India still reveres the bull for its fertility and Shiva, one of the great Hindu gods, is a bull in one of his earthly forms. It is now believed that Shiva is a fusion of the bull-god of the Indus civilization (creator) and the

This impressive sculpture of Nandi stands halfway up Chamundi Hill near Mysore, India. Carved in 1659, from a single granite boulder, Nandi is 7.5m long and 5m high.

bull-god, probably Rudra, of the Aryan civilization (destroyer of cattle and men). Shiva will bestow fertility, but can also destroy.

In a similar fashion to the Apis bull, the priests of Shiva can designate a bull as the living vehicle of the god. The chosen bull is branded on the right hindquarter with a trident symbol (Shiva's weapon of choice) and, because he embodies Shiva, he is universally worshipped. Shiva's vehicle or mount is the sacred milk-white bull called Nandi (literally translated as 'He who pleases'). In Hindu mythology, he is the guardian of all four-legged creatures and also the sentry guard protecting the four corners of the world. Nandi is usually found guarding the entrance of a fertility temple dedicated to Shiva.

BULL RITUALS AND SACRIFICE: MINOAN CRETE

Myths and legends of all early civilizations abound with bulls, and none more so than the Greek myths. A 'who's who' of characters in these myths can be traced back to the bull worship of the Minoan civilization on Crete, which venerated the bull as the father-god symbol.

In a similar fashion to that of Mesopotamia and Egypt, the bull–god–king association existed within Crete. The supreme Greek god Zeus, who possessed irresistible power and uninhibited sexuality, was said to have disguised himself as a magnificent white bull in order to seduce Europa. She was playing by the sea at Tyre with her handmaidens when the bull approached. As he was very tame, Europa dared to climb on his back, at which point Zeus galloped into the sea and swam to Crete. Their union created three sons, including Minos, the

Paolo Veronese, *The Rape of Europa*, 1580, oil on canvas.

Detail from a stone sarcophagus found at Hagia Triada, Crete, showing a trussed-up bull being sacrificed on an altar, c. 1450–1400 BC.

future king of Crete, who would be somewhat haunted by bulls throughout his life (see page 44: 'The Mighty Bull').

The Minoan's worship of the bull centred on certain ritual activities: the spring fertility dances, the bullfights (see 'Spectacular Sport', page 49) and the bull sacrifice. All of these celebrated the bull's strength and fertility. Bulls were sacrificed in Crete to appease many bull-gods, such as Poseidon, the 'Earth-shaker' (god of earthquakes). And particularly in the spring, the sacrificial spilling of bull's blood on to the earth signified the Father-god fertilizing the Earth mother.

Yet not all bull sacrifices were public, solemn and dignified. There were also mystic ceremonies. The Cretans were particularly known for their biennial festival of Zagreus-Dionysus (son of Zeus), who in myth was killed and eaten by the Titans when he was fighting in the form of a bull. Zeus was so enraged that he blasted the Titans with a flash of lightning, and from their ashes arose mankind. Therefore man contains good and bad elements.

During the festival, the devotees or *maenads* ('frenzied ones') would congregate at night in a secluded area and drink wine, dance, scream, shout and take part in orgies. The climax of the event would be the introduction of a young live bull to the proceedings, which the *maenads* would tear apart with their bare hands and teeth. By eating the sacrificial bull, the devotees could obtain mystical union with the god, which would bring them renewed life, fertility and increased strength.

The ritual of sacrifice was not unique to Crete, as it was also practiced by the Sumerians, Egyptians and the peoples of the Levant. The sacrifice of a bull was either meant as a gift to the gods as a method of appeasement, or the sacrifice and resulting feast were a vehicle to transfer the mystical powers of the bull-god to human devotees.

The Calf Bearer: a marble statue found on the site of the Acropolis, of a sacrificial bull-calf offered to Athena, the Protector of Athens, 6th century BC.

ROME

In common with the Minoans, Roman mystic ceremonies often involved the bloody sacrifice of a bull. The worship of the Phrygian god of vegetation, Attis, and his lover Cybele (the goddess of fertility), was adopted by the Romans in AD 204. According to myth, Attis castrated himself so as to offer his vitality to Cybele and bled to death under a pine tree, but spring flowers sprung up from his blood. The Romans held an annual ceremony in the spring to mourn his death and rejoice in his resurrection.

But in secret, the devotees of Attis performed a *taurobolium*, which baptized or initiated them into a cult:

> . . . the devotee, crowned with gold and wreathed with fillets, descended into a pit, the mouth of which was covered with a wooden grating. A bull, adorned with

The Roman god Mithras killing the sacrificial bull, marble, 2nd century AD.

garlands of flowers, its forehead glittering with gold leaf, was then driven on to the grating and there stabbed to death with a consecrated spear. Its hot reeking blood poured in torrents through the apertures, and was received with devout eagerness by the worshipper on every part of his person and garments, till he emerged from the pit, drenched, dripping, and scarlet from head to foot, to receive the homage, nay the adoration, of his fellows as one who had been born again to eternal life and had washed away his sins in the blood of the bull.[8]

Another god taken over by the Romans was the Persian god of light, Mithra. He was said to have attacked and killed the 3000-year-old primeval bull, Geush Urvan, and from the blood and semen of the bull sprung all animals and plants. Mithra ate the flesh of the bull with the sun god, Sol, while they sat on the bull's skin. The Romans renamed the god Mithras in 67 BC, and Mithraism reached its peak in AD 308, when it was declared the official religion of the Roman army. This was a secret male cult, especially entrenched in the military, and many of its rituals were held in caves, away from prying eyes.[9] Mithras was regarded as the god of light, justice and truth, and by feasting on bull's flesh, the initiates would be able to triumph over their adversaries; giving them a moral victory over evil, and assuring them of salvation in this world, and in the afterlife.

CHRISTIANS AND CELTS

With bull worship so firmly entrenched in the psyche of so many civilizations, the Christian Church found it hard to change people's affiliation. According to the Bible, the bull worship in Israel had to be wiped out: there was the supreme god of the Canaanites, El and Baal to contest. These bull-gods were repre-

Celtic admiration for the bull is shown on the 'Gundestrup Cauldron' found in Denmark in 1891, which depicts a ritual bull sacrifice or hunt. Embossed silver-gilt, 1st century BC.

sented by the idol of the Golden Calf/Bull which Aaron built at the bottom of Mount Sinai, while the Israelites waited for Moses to return from God with the Ten Commandments. Bull cults were branded as sexually perverse, full of false doctrine and weird practices.

The ancient Celts were particularly resistant to change as the Druids (the religious priests of the Celts) used bulls as sacrificial offerings. Pliny the Elder wrote lyrically about the Druids sacrificing a pair of white bulls as a gift to the gods, when mistletoe was found growing on sacred oak trees. The mistletoe, when taken in a potion, was believed to increase cattle fertility, and the plant was an antidote to all poisons affecting humans and cattle.[10]

Another Celtic ritual was that of the *tarbhfheis* ('bull-sleep'), which was used at Tara, during the installation of the High King of Ireland. A bull, usually with yellow skin, would be sacrificed and one Druid would feast on the flesh and drink a broth made from the animal. He would then go into trance, or sleep, wrapped in the sacrificed bull's hide. During this sleep he would receive a vision of the next true king.[11]

It was no coincidence that at the council of Toledo in 447, when the Christian Church published its first official description of the Devil, it was apparently part-bull:

> . . . a large black monstrous apparition with horns on his head, cloven hoofs – or one cloven hoof – ass's ears, hair, claws, fiery eyes, terrible teeth, an immense phallus, and a sulphurous smell.[12]

THE MIGHTY BULL AS ADVERSARY

Although bull-gods did eventually disappear, the image of the bull as a mighty adversary has lived on to this day. Anyone who

Bulls fighting on an 18th Dynasty Egyptian ostrakon (c. 1550–1290 BC).

has witnessed the sight of two adult male bulls fighting during the mating season will have an idea of their strength and power.

In the Celtic legend of the *Táin Bó Cuailnge* (Cattle Raid of Cooley), the Donn Cuailnge, the Brown Bull of Cooley, was an extremely fertile stud bull belonging to Ulster. He was strong, virile and an object of wealth and desire: a status symbol which the rest of Ireland wanted to own. The following passage describes the strength and ferocity of the Brown Bull as he attacks another one, the White-Horned Bull of Connaught:

> And he fought the White-horned, and tore him limb from limb, and carried off pieces of him on his horns, dropping the loins at Athlone and the liver at Trim. Then he went back to Cualgne, and turned mad, killing all who crossed his path, until his heart burst with bellowing, and he fell dead.[13]

More realistically, the following passage from *The Georgics* (29 BC) – written by the Roman poet Virgil – is perhaps the best poetic portrayal of a young bull challenging a dominant bull for supremacy, and his eventual victory:

> While with charge and countercharge they fight it out,
> The blood from many wounds darkening their sides.
> Crashes are heard as they fling themselves together;
> A furious bellowing fills woods and sky.
> They cannot share a stable. One or the other
> Must yield, broken in the fight, and withdraw far off,
> Taking with him the injury and shame of defeat;
> The love he has lost belongs to his proud conqueror;
> One last look back and he goes like a banished king.
> Through days and nights of exile, brooding his return,
> He hardens himself with rough living, a bed of stones,
> A diet of sharp-edged rushes and prickly leaves.
> He learns how to make his horns declare his fury
> And tests himself, butting treetrunks, slashing the air,
> Pawing up the ground as if battle had begun.
> Once he has recovered strength he advances again:
> He rushes his enemy, catching him off guard,
> Like a wave which begins to whiten far out at sea,
> Gathering behind it the lifted force of waters
> As it curls shoreward and roars across the rocks,
> A fluid mountain that tears itself from its base
> To topple and break in eddies of black sand.[14]

It is obvious from this description why the might and fury of the bull made him a supreme opponent for the heroes in Greek mythology. Jason has to yoke two fire-breathing, bronze-footed bulls to obtain the Golden Fleece, and Heracles and Theseus have to contend with several destructive and savage bulls.[15]

Heracles' first encounter was during his seventh labour, when he was dispatched to Crete to capture and remove the sea-born Cretan Bull. This white bull had been sent by Poseidon as a divine sign of Minos' right to succeed his 'adoptive' father's throne. But Minos failed to sacrifice this bull to Poseidon, because it was so dazzlingly beautiful. As part of Minos' punishment, the angry god sent the Cretan Bull mad. It turned into a savage, fire-breathing beast which devastated the whole of Crete, spoiling crops and knocking down orchard walls.

Heracles managed to catch hold of the bull by its horns and vault on to its back, where, despite being bucked, he stayed on and rode it until it became broken like a horse. He then rode the

Adrien Voisard-Margerie, *Bulls Fighting (Rivalry)*, 1923, pastel on paper.

Theseus slitting the throat of the Minotaur; painted Greek ceramic vase, 600–501 BC.

bull into the sea and across to the Greek mainland. The bull was turned loose, but reverting to its old ways, it started to rampage across the plains of Marathon towards Athens. Eventually, the Athenian hero Theseus was called in to overpower it and drag it to Athens, where the fire-breathing and murderous bull was sacrificed to Apollo.

As well as sending the Cretan Bull mad, Poseidon also caused King Minos' wife, Pasiphae, to fall madly in love with the creature. To satisfy her desires, she persuaded the craftsman Daedalus to build her a decoy cow, made of wood and covered with hide. She climbed inside the decoy and arranged herself so that when the Cretan Bull mounted the cow he also mated with her. The result was the monstrous half-bull, half-man, known as the Minotaur.

This creature was housed in the Labyrinth built by Daedalus at Knossos, and every nine years seven boys and seven girls were sent from Athens to the Labyrinth as food for the monster. However, one year Theseus volunteered to be in the sacrifice

party. Instead of being the victim, he stole into the Labyrinth and killed the sleeping Minotaur.

How to capture a wild bull, according to the gold Vaphio cups, c. 1500 BC

SPECTACULAR SPORT

These myths seem to have been based on fact, because in Crete there was a tradition of people demonstrating their skills in the dangerous sport of bull-leaping. Although the sport probably had a religious aspect, it was also enjoyed as a highly entertaining spectacle.[16] The bulls used for the fights may have been specially bred, having their speed and wits dulled. They were probably kept semi-wild on ranches and then caught. Two possible methods used to capture them for the ring can be seen on embossed gold cups from about 1500 BC, found at Vaphio near Sparta (although they were Minoan or Cretan in origin). One shows a wild bull being driven into a large net stretched between trees, and then having his legs tied together for transport into town. The other shows a rather unsporting scene of a tame cow being used as a decoy to attract the wild bull, whose back legs are then tied together when he is distracted.

While Minoan bull-sports are the best known, there is evidence of similar acrobatic feats in Cappadocia (south-east Asia

49

Bull-leaping fresco, Palace of Knossos, Crete, 1700–1500 BC: The man is leaping over the bull's back, while two women act as a bull-grappler and a catcher.

Minor) and in Anatolia (Turkey). In one shrine at Catal Huyuk in Turkey, a mural portrays a man jumping on the back of an enormous bull six feet long; part of the man's loincloth is caught on the bull's horns.

There is another bull sport shown on a number of Minoan seals, which can only be described as bull-wrestling. It is an image associated with Heracles and Theseus subduing the Cretan Bull. The man, on foot, grasps the bull by the muzzle and by the horns, twists its head around and tries to throw it to the ground.

This feat was replicated by cowboys in the Wild West shows of 1880s America; jumping from their horses on to the bull's back. In today's rodeo, the spectacle has been turned into an event known as bull- or steer-dogging. The other bull-related event from the early days of rodeo is bull-riding, which finally

Matt Morgan, 'Cowboy Life Riding a Yearling', 1888, wood engraving (from a photograph by C. D. Kirkland), on the cover of *Frank Leslie's Illustrated Newspaper*, 5 May 1988.

became a stand-alone sport in America in 1992, with the formation of Professional Bull Riders, Inc. (PBR). It is now a multi-million-dollar business, with events spread across America, Brazil, Canada and Australia.

The bulls are specially bred to have the desire and ability to buck wildly. In 2003, the sport was voted the most dangerous contest in America – for the competitor, not the bull. The rider's aim (as it has always been) is to stay on the bull for eight seconds,[17] holding on to a strap around the bull's neck with one hand.

Their eventual score partly rests on the judges' scoring of the bull's bucking performance, and the bull is the wild card of the event – on some outings they are mellow, at other times extremely dangerous. One of the most famous bulls was Red Rock, who bucked off every one of the 309 riders who tried to ride him between 1984 and 1987. Eventually, he was conquered by the World Champion Bull Rider of 1987, Lane Frost, in May 1988.

Neither of the rodeo events mentioned are connected to real life cowboy tasks; they are just spectacular entertainment.[18] Professional riders such as J. W. Hart speak of the thrill and adrenaline rush they get when facing the bull:

> There just ain't a rush like getting on a 2,000 lb bull. It gets your heart racing. Once you nod for them to open the shoot gate, there's no backing out. You think about staying on, nothing else. When a bull jumps, you've got to counter that, but at the speed they're going, there's no way you can think that fast and keep up for eight seconds. Eight seconds is a long time on the back of a bull.[19]

Ordinary people have flocked to Pamplona in Spain for centuries to experience the same thrill of facing a bull. The Running of the Bulls during the Fiesta da San Fermín (7–14 July) is mentioned in accounts of the festival from the seventeenth century onwards, when the moving of the bulls from their corrals to the bullring became part of the entertainment.[20] Volunteers who wish to run with the bulls wear red bandannas or scarves round their necks, and the bravest souls carry a rolled-up newspaper, which is nicknamed the Pamplona Badge of Honour. It indicates their intention to get closest to the bull, and if they are unable to touch the bull with their 'badge', they feel their honour is lost.

If all goes smoothly, the bull run lasts two to three minutes, but sometimes a bull becomes separated from the pack and becomes confused, swings round, tosses his head, and furiously attacks anyone in his way. Ernest Hemingway in his novel *The Sun Also Rises* (1926), originally titled *Fiesta*, describes the goring to death of one of the runners:

> I saw the bulls just coming out of the street into the long running pen. They were going fast and gaining on the crowd. Just then another drunk started out from the fence with a blouse in his hands. He wanted to do capework with the bulls. The two policemen tore out, collared him, one hit him with a club, and they dragged him against the fence and stood flattened out against the fence as the last of the crowd and the bulls went by. There were so many people running ahead of the bulls that the mass thickened and slowed up going through the gate into the ring, and as the bulls passed, galloping together, heavy, muddy-sided, horns swinging, one shot ahead, caught a man in the running crowd in the back and lifted him in the air. Both the man's arms were by his sides, his head went back as the horns went in, and the bull lifted him and then dropped him. The bull picked another man running in front, but the man disappeared into the crowd, and the crowd was through the gate and into the ring with the bulls behind them.[21]

Since record-keeping began in 1924, fourteen people have been killed during the Pamplona runs and over 200 gored. The last death was in 1995, when a young American was killed on the horns of a bull.

Purple Fury: the colourful event of Jallikattu, held annually in Madurai, India.

BULL SPORTS IN ASIA

The Asian equivalent of the Pamplona bull-running is the South Indian sport of *Jallikattu* or *Manchu Virattu* ('chasing the bull'). The annual event is played out in the villages of Tamil Nadu, on the third day of the Pongal Festival (harvest thanksgiving), on which day the cattle are celebrated. The object of Jallikattu is to 'tame' an agitated and drunken bull running in the open or in an enclosed space by gaining control over its horns, neck or tail. Traditionally, the contest winner was assured of snaring a bride after showing off his valour and skills against the wild bull.[22]

No less dangerous is bull-racing, which is a popular rural sport in Pakistan, Bali, in the Punjab region of India and on Madura, an island in Indonesia. The sport is thought to have evolved centuries ago from plough teams racing across barren fields; and on Madura it was a sporting passion of the early king of Sumenep, one of the island's towns. A pair of zebu bulls are yoked together and dressed up with gaudy decorations. They are often fed a special 'racing' diet of grains, pulses and grass, and given a mixture of ginger, pepper, chillis, honey, beer and eggs to enliven them even more. The aim of the race is for the 'jockey' to stand on a metal board or cart behind the bulls as they career off, hopefully in a straight line, for two kilometres, only holding on to the bulls' tails or a pair of reins which are attached to the yoke.[23]

The other bull sport in Asia does not involve humans; just the head-to-head combat of two bulls. Annual contests take place in Thailand and South Korea, where bulls are specially trained and fed for the event. Whereas today the owner of the winning bull (the one who stands his ground) receives money, traditionally the prize was the season's best grazing ground.[24]

BULLS VERSUS OTHER ANIMALS

While the sports mentioned tend to glorify the bull, humans have also invented combats that cast the bull in a darker role, often fighting to the death against other animals.

Bulls played a major role in the Roman *venationes*, or hunting games. They were pitted against elephants at the *Circus Maximus* in Rome in 79 BC and later with tigers, rhinoceroses, wild boar and lions. Fights to the death between animals symbolized the struggles of the jungle and were 'illustrative of the primal chaos of the natural world'.[25] Seneca (4 BC–AD 65), the Roman philosopher and dramatist, tells of a bull and panther that were chained together; they ripped each other to shreds before they were finally put out of their misery.

Whereas the Romans used bulls to recreate the spectacular violence of nature, the English baited the bull before it was

Bull-baiting scene from Edward Jesse, *Anecdotes of Dogs* (1846).

slaughtered to tenderize its flesh. Although baiting a bull with dogs was the national sport of England between the thirteenth and nineteenth centuries, the 'sport' began as a misguided culinary practice.[26] Ironically, the distress of the animal would make its flesh 'tougher'.

Butchers had their own dogs which they would send out to round up a bull from the field, chase it and 'throw' (pin) it to the ground. Once the bull was chained to a stake the dogs would be set at it, one by one. These specially bred dogs – bulldogs – were tenacious and brave. They would aim to 'pin and hold' the bull's nose, its most tender part, which would render it helpless. The bull would retaliate by trying to get its horns under the dogs' bellies and throw them into the air.

The public developed a taste for this violent and cruel event. Baiting occurred at country fairs and wakes, and in ale-house courtyards where local dogs would be invited to challenge travelling bulls. Bets were taken on the outcome: the 'bull's eye', a crown piece in circulation during the early 1800s, was often placed on the outcome of a bait. Most towns had a bull/bear ring, commonly known as a 'bear garden', and in eighteenth-century London bull baiting took place twice a week at Hockley-in-the-Hole, Clerkenwell, at Marylebone Fields, Soho, and at Tothill Fields, Westminster.[27] The bulls were paraded through the streets before the baiting. John Gay in *Trivia* (1716) describes the scene in the notoriously dangerous and unruly area of Hockley-in-the-Hole:

> . . . led by the Nostrill walkes the muzzled Beare
> Behinde him moves majestically dull
> The Pride of Hockley-hole, the surly Bull . . .[28]

An added entertainment, described in *The Weekly Journal* of 9 June 1716, was a wild bull 'with fireworks stuck all over him', turned loose and chased through the streets. Spectators were asked to arrive at about three o'clock, 'because this sport continues long'.[29]

A similar type of event happened annually in Stamford, Lincolnshire, and Tutbury in Staffordshire, where it was known as 'The Bull Running'. The bull would have its ears cropped, its tail cut down to a stump, its body smeared with soap and pepper blown up its nostrils. Then, in a maddened state, it would be turned loose and everyone would try to catch him.

Far from being a pastime solely for the 'mob', bull-baiting was enjoyed even by royalty. Elizabeth I was known to organize bull-baits for visiting dignitaries at Whitehall and she even visited the public baits held at Paris Garden on Bankside.

Early attempts to ban bull-baiting were futile, mainly due to the authorities' requirement to improve the quality of meat, and it was not unusual for a newly elected provincial Mayor to provide the citizens with a bull for baiting. When the first Parliamentary proposal was made to abolish bull-baiting in a bill sent before the House of Commons by Sir William Pulteney in 1800, hardly any politicians bothered to turn up. *The Times*, which reported the bill's defeat, hailed the issue as 'beneath the dignity of Parliament', and the future Prime Minister George Canning defended the sport on the grounds that 'the amusement inspired courage and produced a nobleness of sentiment and elevation of mind'.[30]

Eventually in 1835 the baiting of bulls was made illegal – though not because of cruelty towards the bulls, but because the baits threatened social order. The law-makers (often gentleman who themselves liked to frequent the baits) were more concerned about the effects of the bloody spectacle on the lower orders, who preferred watching bull-baits to working. It was now felt that watching these violent baits encouraged, and vindicated, cruelty towards humanity.[31]

FIGHTS TO THE DEATH: MAN VERSUS BULL

Returning to the Roman amphitheatre, another contest pitted man against bull in a fight to the death. Being a familiar symbol of savagery in the Mediterranean world, the bull was an ideal animal enemy for Romans to fight and conquer. Pliny the Elder describes these fighting bulls in *The Natural History*:

> The bull has a proud air, a stern forehead, shaggy ears, and horns which appear always ready, and challenging to the combat; but it is by his fore feet that he manifests his threatening anger. As his rage increases, he stands, lashing back his tail every now and then, and throwing up the

sand against his belly; being the only animal that excites himself by these means.[32]

Specialist bullfighters called *taurarii* fought on foot with lances and pikes. Julius Caesar introduced unarmed fighters on horseback in 45 BC, an idea he borrowed from the people of Thessaly (now Macedonia). The horsemen would chase the bull around the arena until they were exhausted; at this point the fighter would jump from the horse on to the bull's back and attempt to wrestle it to the ground by twisting its neck.

The world of Roman *venationes* is a far cry from the modern bullring. Although the end result is the same (the bloody death of the bull), the commercialized *corrida* (bullfight) is anything but a sport, as it is not a fair contest – is it a spectacle, ritual, ceremony, a sacrifice or art?[33] Pablo Picasso, an aficionado of bullfighting from a very young age, declared the *corrida* an art: 'It is rare to find an art that is so intelligent about itself', he told his art dealer after visiting Nîmes (one of the French centres of bullfighting) in 1912.[34]

Bullfighting has been an elite Spanish social institution at least since the Middle Ages. In about 1090 the hero El Cid in the *Poem of the Cid* fought bulls at the marriage of his two daughters. Ordinary Spaniards have incorporated bullfighting (though not to the death) into some of their rituals, mainly those relating to marriage. A late nineteenth-century ritual in rural Spain began two days before a wedding. The groom and his friends would run a bull through the town, taunting it with their jackets. When they reached the fiancée's house, the groom would thrust a pair of darts, which had been decorated by his fiancée, into the bull's back, the idea being that the sexual potency of the bull could be transferred to the newlyweds.[35] In 1726, Francisco Romero introduced the modern bullfight: the matador fought

Francisco de Goya, *La Tauromaquia*, plate 1: 'How the ancient Spanish hunted bulls on horseback in the countryside', 1816, etching and aquatint.

Francisco de Goya, *La Tauromaquia*, plate 19 'More of his [Martincho] craziness in the same bullring', 1816, etching and aquatint.

on foot rather than on horseback, and was equipped with a cape (*muleta*) and sword, which allowed the bull to be killed from the front, with a single thrust.

The history of Spanish bullfighting, beginning with the hunting of bulls in open country, is captured in the 33 etchings which make up Goya's *Tauromaquia*, published in 1816.[36] Although they are part-memoir and part-fantasy, the images reveal the showbiz side of the bullring: the famous matadors and their amazing performance stunts.

FIGHTING BULLS

What makes a good fighting bull can be described by two words – *bravura* (wildness or ferocity) and *nobleza* (honest and straight charges, predictability). The bulls, to be worthy competitors, need to show pure aggression, endurance and a limitless pain barrier.

From the late eighteenth century onwards, when the number of *corridas* increased, specialist breeders began to breed bulls selectively to meet demand, and also to avoid the effects of domestication, which were threatening to dilute the bulls' wildness. Previously, event organizers contacted their local butcher to provide suitably fierce bulls from those intended for domestic slaughter.[37]

Today, bulls with a target weight of 500–600 kg are carefully reared for four years on ranches (*ganaderias*): they are deliberately bred to kill or be killed. And although it is a pedigree animal, it will only ever be in the arena once. Spectators, rather than seeing an individual animal, only remember a good, bad or indifferent type of bull – unless, of course, it manages to kill a matador: then it becomes famous.[38]

The popular image of the dangerous bull, with its head lowered, pawing the ground before attacking is a universal one, still beloved of Hollywood film, cartoons and school playgrounds. But any fighting bull exhibiting this behaviour in the modern Spanish bullring is classed as cowardly – although it is a threatening action, the bull is hesitant and not sure of its attack.

During the *corrida* the bull goes through three physical and emotional stages. First, the *toro bravo* (wild bull) enters the arena. He is strong, proud and spoiling for a fight. The matador takes him through some preliminary movements, called *suerte de capote* ('act of cape'). He charges wildly and freely at the cape; the proverbial 'bull in a china shop'. Like the champion boxer Jake La Motta, played by Robert de Niro in the film *Raging Bull* (1980), he is full of rage and violence, emotions which make him virtually unstoppable in the ring.

Most depictions of the bullfight show the next stage of the *corrida:* the bull's contact with the mounted *picadors*. Although the horses are heavily armoured and blindfolded, traditionally the horses were unprotected, and bore the brunt of the bull's anger: Picasso, Goya and Manet all captured the gory mess made of the picadors' horses.

At the end of this confrontation the bull appears to have won as the horses leave the arena. He is left alone. But then, as Hemingway notes in *Death in The Afternoon* (1932):

Lake Price, *Chulos Playing the Bull*, 1860–70, lithograph. A *Chulo* (roughly 'dandy') is the bullfighter's assistant.

In the second act he is baffled completely by an unarmed man and very cruelly punished by the *banderillas* [harpoon-shaped darts] so that his confidence and his blind rage go and he concentrates his hatred on an individual object . . . When the *banderillas* are in he is done for. They are the sentencing. The first act is the trial, the second act is the sentencing and the third the execution.[39]

A good bull will be slowed by the *banderillas*, but he is probably at his most dangerous because he now recognizes his enemy. He is aiming his attacks. He is still brave and strong.

Édouard Manet, *Bullfight*, 1865–6, oil on canvas. In modern bullfighting the horses may be blindfolded and covered by latticed padding, but they are still viewed by the bull as the natural enemy.

'The *Espada* (swordsman) meeting the plunging bull, buries the sword in his shoulder': Dealing the fatal blow at a bull-fight in Seville, Spain, c. 1902, stereographic photograph.

The final act is the matador dominating the bull with the *muleta*. This act is designed to wear down the bull until he knows he has lost the battle. The bull's head will lower, he will lose his speed and he becomes heavy and tired. The execution – the 'moment of truth' or *estocada* – when it is performed correctly, should see the matador going over the bull's horns to thrust his sword between the arches of the bull's shoulder-blades.

It appears that the 'heroic' matador has confronted death purposefully, even gracefully, and by his control, skill and actions has outwitted the bull. But the *muleta* will only protect the matador if the bull has never faced a man before. If he has, then the matador is as good as dead. This is why a fighting bull never enters the bullring twice.

PROVOKING EMOTIONS

Rather than depicting the death of the bull, most artists have tended to capture the vivid theatre of the bullfight, and also the bull's victories. Goya's *The Death of a Picador* (1793), part of a

64

series of eight bullfighting studies, shows the bull goring the picador's horse and the picador himself.

The bullfight, and its symbolism, was a familiar part of Picasso's work throughout his life, but most markedly from the mid-1930s. He used the violence of the bullfight (the bull symbolizing masculinity, the horse of femininity) to try and vent the rage, guilt and desire that dogged him in his private life during his secret affair with Marie-Thérèse, while married to Olga: he is also the Minotaur in his *Minotauromachie* series.[40] But probably Picasso's most famous depiction of a bull is in *Guernica* (1937), which he painted as a response to the tragedy of the Nazi German-led bombing of the town of Guernica on 26 April 1937 during the Spanish Civil War. Although he never definitively explained the painting's symbolism, the bull could stand for the Spanish people, standing defiantly against the aggressors, or he could be a symbol of the brutality and darkness of war and fascism.

Progressing from canvas to celluloid, the bullfight, with its potential for spectacle, was the subject of one of the earliest films, shot in Madrid in 1895 by Francis Doublier. The footage, which was shown at the Grand Café in Paris, includes parts of the parade and the fight, the sudden charges and threats of the bull, and the matador attempting the kill.

The later film *A Spanish Bullfight* (1900) was subject to censorship in Britain on the grounds of animal cruelty. The stark black-and-white images, played out in silence, show the demise of the bull without the usual background of crowd noise, intense emotion and warm sunshine: the brutal fight to the death.[41]

The bullring has also been used to illustrate a simple moral: peace and gentleness are better than fighting and death. The character of Ferdinand the Bull was created by Munro Leaf in his bestselling book, published in 1936. Ferdinand is a gentle, peace-loving bull who, when forced into the Madrid bull-ring, only wants to sit down and sniff the scent of the flower bouquets which the lady spectators have thrown at the matadors. The story was turned into an award-winning Disney cartoon, *Ferdinand the Bull* (1938).

Aside from Spain, bulls are regularly fought in France, Portugal and in the Latin American republics of Colombia, Ecuador, Guatemala, Mexico, Panama, Peru and Venezuela. There is even a bullfighting school in San Diego, California. However, in 2004 Barcelona declared itself 'an anti-bullfighting city' following a series of public protests and a petition. Another 38 Catalan municipalities have followed suit, and in December 2006 it was anounced that the last bullring in Barcelona is to close after a fall in visitor numbers. It is thought that Barcelona is a good 'yardstick' for all cultural trends across the country: the *corrida* may be lost forever in Spain.

3 Cow Mysticism and a Rural Idyll

As in nature, the attributes of the cow and her associated symbolism are the direct opposite of those of the bull. While he is linked with strength and power, she radiates gentleness. He bellows; she lows. He is feared; she is loved.

There is probably no other animal surrounded by such poetic associations and rural idealism as the cow: the gentle caresses of the pure milkmaid are needed to bring on her milk and she is a source of solace from the urban bustle; she provides 'relaxation for the tired'.[1] And there is also no other animal so closely associated to the human female: cows are mothers, beautiful girls, aristocratic leaders and downtrodden women.

RESPECT FOR THE COW

Until recently, humans throughout the world have respected and treated the cow well – for she was (and still is in pastoral cultures) the epitome of usefulness. Without complaint and in a gentle manner, she provides male calves for use in the fields, nourishes humans with milk and milk products, and provides manure for fuel and fertilizing of crops. She is the ultimate provider of inexhaustible riches. And as a bulky and expensive animal to keep, she has been looked after and petted – she is a

A weeping cow allowing her milk to be taken to feed man, rather than her calf, Egypt, 11th Dynasty (2134–1991 BC).

precious commodity. As the English courtier and scientist Sir Kenelm Digby wrote in 1658:

> there's not the meanest cottager but hath a cow to furnish his family with milk; 'tis the principal sustenance of the poorest sort of people . . . which makes them very careful of the good keeping and health of their cows.[2]

She is an everyday sort of animal: neither exotic nor exciting, just there and always providing, living quite happily alongside humans. It seems rather a contradiction, then, that an animal so passive and forbearing became such a huge star of global folklore and ancient mythology. But a passage in the novel *The Cow* (1999) by Beat Sterchi seems to sum up the reason: respect.

The Spanish herdsman, Ambrosio, who is used to the 'pride and the nimble rage of a young bull from Coruña', takes charge of a herd of twelve Simmental dairy cows in Switzerland. He is unable to admire the cows, but

. . . he couldn't deny that these overbred bodies had something reassuringly decent about them, it might well be dull, but the warmth they radiated, their incessant inner activity, their endless ruminating, digesting, multiplying, lactating, producing-even-while-they-slept, all that impressed Ambrosio in spite of himself. Sometimes their uninterrupted productivity seemed positively god-like to him, and he learned to respect it.[3]

The cow symbolizes maternal nourishment because of her ability to provide milk. In effect, she is the Mother of humans, and by inference also of the gods. Her milking ability is her passport to greatness. There is nothing more to her: milk is her *raison d'être*, as simply put by the American poet Ogden Nash (1902–1971):

The cow is of the bovine ilk;
One end is moo, the other, milk.[4]

The house cow provided the household's entire dairy needs, photograph of c. 1902.

While cow-goddesses are often the consorts of bull-gods (as seen in Mesopotamia), she takes centre stage in several creation myths. Audhumla is the primeval cow in Nordic mythology known as the 'nourisher', who provides four rivers of milk for the evil frost-giant Ymir, whose body parts eventually form the world. She herself feeds on the salt which covers the ice-blocks in the great abyss (Ginnungagap) which is full of latent energy awaiting creation. Over the course of three days, she licks at the salty blocks until the first human man appears, called Buri. He has a son called Bor, who in turn has three sons. They hate Ymir so they attack and kill him. With his body they make the earth, the sea from his blood and the sky from his skull. Audhumla is therefore also known as the creative force.

The Egyptians, according to Herodotus in *An Account of Egypt*, did not sacrifice or eat the flesh of cows, as they were sacred to their cow-goddesses. Neith, the great primeval mother whose cult centre was at Sais, was similar to Audhumla. The fullest account of her part in creation is written on the temple walls at Esna. At the beginning of time she appears as a cow, Ihet, floating on the Nun (a watery mass of dark, directionless chaos). By invoking their names, she forms thirty primeval gods who have to help her in her creation. She starts by giving birth to the sun-god, Ra, and is therefore the Mother of all gods.

In later times, the Egyptians had several different cow-goddesses – Nut, Hathor and Isis.[5] The sky-goddess Nut is sometimes depicted as a cow, for this is the form she assumes when she bears Ra on her back up to the sky. The dutiful cow gets obediently to her feet, but rises so high that she becomes dizzy. Four gods are appointed to support her legs (which became the four pillars of the sky). Shu, god of the air, holds up her belly, which

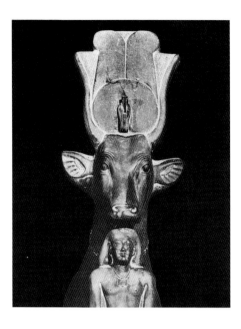

Hathor as a cow, watching over the Pharaoh Psammetichus I, 572–525 BC.

becomes the firmament to which Ra attaches the stars and the constellations to light the earth.

In one myth Nut gives birth to Ra daily and he passes over her body until he reaches her mouth at sunset. He then passes into her mouth and through her body, and is reborn the next morning.

The mother-goddess *par excellence* of Egyptian gods is Hathor, and when she is at her most nurturing and protecting she is depicted in her cow form. Hathor became goddess of motherhood, gaining titles such as 'The Great Cow Who Protects Her Child'. Her priests (male and female) were oracles and midwives, and Hathor's protection could be invoked over children and pregnant women. In connection with Isis, she provides sustenance for the souls of the dead in the Underworld during their mummification, and when their hearts are being weighed in the Judgement Hall. She is also depicted in cow form as the Mistress of the Theban Necropolis.

Mythology, therefore, places the cow at the centre of the universe and as Mother of humans and gods. Folklore, on the other hand, tends to depict the cow in her normal role as continuous provider, albeit in a respectfully magical way.

In Celtic folklore there are cows who will magically appear before any deserving person in need of their milk, supplying a never-ending amount for free: the brindled black-and-brown magic Welsh cow *Fuwch Frech*, and *Glas Ghaibhneach*, the grey cow of Irish tradition.[6] However, the cows will soon disappear if they are struck, milked into a leaky bucket or otherwise offended. The Dun Cow – a gigantic beast belonging to a giant and kept on Mitchell Fold in Shropshire – reacted in a particularly violent way when she was expected to provide more milk than she wanted to. As with most mythical cows, her milk supply was inexhaustible, but one day an old woman who had already filled her milk bucket, wanted also to fill her leaking bucket, therefore wasting precious milk. This so enraged the cow that she broke loose from the fold and wandered onto Dunsmore Heath, where she was said to have haunted a ditch and savagely injured many people. She was eventually slain by the heroic Guy, Earl of Warwick.

Another cow steeped in (negative) folklore is Daisy, the cow belonging to the Irish immigrant Kate O'Leary, who became a legend of the silver screen. Daisy was supposed to have started the Great Chicago Fire on 8 October 1871 after kicking over a kerosene lamp. Even though Michael Ahern, the reporter who created the cow story, admitted in 1893 that he had made it up, the tale become an urban myth and was depicted in the film *In Old Chicago* (1935). Chicago became known as 'The City That a Cow Kicked Over'.[7]

Another rural myth concerning cows has recently been exposed by researchers in Canada. The idea that you can tip over a cow using brute strength, known as cow-tipping, is a fallacy. It is often cited as a drunken entertainment in the countryside, reports *The Times*, to 'sneak up on an unsuspecting cow and turn the poor animal hoof over udder'.[8]

NATURALLY AGGRESSIVE COWS

They appear to go against the grain, but naturally aggressive cows do exist, and indeed are often celebrated. At the end of the daily bull runs in Pamplona, when the bulls are safely held in corrals, the amateurs congregate waiting for the *vaquilla*. This event sees the release of five fighting cows into the ring, allowing a brush with danger, without confronting a bull.

The raging cow played a part in the martyrdom of Perpetua, one of the many patron saints of cattle. She was put into a Roman amphitheatre against a mad heifer for preaching Christianity. The story goes that she was tossed by the heifer, but got up and helped her slave, Felicitas, who was also in the arena. Perpetua killed herself with a gladiator's sword, rather than being despatched unwillingly.

Another breed of naturally aggressive cow is the Herens breed (sometimes known as the Eringer breed), which come from the Swiss Canton of Valais. They instinctively engage in duels to determine the hierarchy for leading the herd to its Alpine summer pastures. Since 1923, organized competitions have seen huge crowds gather to watch regional bouts between specially bred cows, with the 'Queen of the Herd' or 'Cantonal Queen' eventually crowned in May at the finals held in Aproz. Calves born to the Queen will be worth at least $3,600.[9]

Herens cows battling for supremacy during the spring competitions at Raron, in the Swiss canton of Valais.

While the Herens cows are not particularly dangerous to humans, there is always a risk involved when working with cattle: it is a dangerous occupation. According to the British Health and Safety Executive, between 1994 and 1999 23 people were killed by cattle, with hundreds of others injured. Incidents involving cows are most likely when their maternal instinct is aroused to protect their calves from 'dangerous' people.[10]

THE SACRED COW

Not surprisingly, India is home to the greatest concentration of cows in the world and in Hindu India we find an overwhelming abundance of cow-love. Like many countries, India has its own mythical cow, Surabhi, who is known as the 'Cow of Plenty' (and also as Kamadhenu, the 'Wish-Fulfilling Cow'); she is the first of the treasures to emerge from the primeval ocean of milk churned by Vishnu, and is believed to be the mother of all cows.

Hindus' daily lives are full of rituals, practices and habits which revolve around the cow. Cows are worshipped at festivals,

Feeding a sacred cow: averting evils and fulfilling your wishes.

and in some parts of India a special day in November called *Gosthastami* is set aside for the cow. The bulls of Shiva roam the streets unmolested, and cow's milk, curds and ghee are used in temple rituals as offerings to the gods. The heady liquid known as *Pancha-gavya* is a solution made from the five products of the live cow: milk, ghee, curds, urine and dung. It is the most potent and sacred substance known to Hindus and it is ascribed magical and purification properties, such as averting evil and bestowing blessings on marriages.

So how and from where did the concept of the sacred cow arise? Although there is no evidence of the cow being sacred in the Indus Valley, the cow was certainly linked to the Mother Goddess, who was herself the cow providing milk as the life-bestowing agent. But the cow becomes central to Indian society during the Vedic period: cows are the mothers of the universe. In the *Rig-Veda*, the cow is associated with Prithivi (the Mother Earth) who is consort to Dyava (the Heavens). The mother of the gods, Aditi, is called the 'Milch-cow'[11] and cows symbolize life-giving substances such as rain clouds, and the cosmic waters from which the universe is created.[12]

Despite the esteem and affection bestowed on the cow, she was not viewed by the Aryans as sacred and inviolable in her own right. She was sacrificed to the gods, with her flesh ritually eaten by the Brahman priests at funeral rites (men would be wrapped in her hide to protect them on their journey) and on other occasions, such as the building of a new house.

It was not until late medieval times, when the principle of *ahimsa* became widespread – the Hindu, Buddhist and Jainist moral and ethical doctrine of non-injury and compassion – that the cow was regarded as totally sacred and the thought of killing the surrogate mother of the human race became repugnant. But although the concept of *ahimsa* was probably introduced to India around the sixth century BC, it took time to break down Brahmanical rule and change society's behaviour.

The abolition of cow sacrifice and the avoidance of beef was firmly entrenched in Hindu India before the Moslem invasions of the eleventh century, but the introduction of Islamic culture to India only served to strengthen the cow's sanctity. The Moslem invaders were beef-eaters and 'cow killers'; thus the cow became a symbol of Hindu culture, and the chief reason for Hindu resistance against the spread of Islam. In a similar fashion, resentment against Moghul India, and the British presence in India, contributed to the cause of cow-protection. Even today, there are clashes between Hindus and Moslems over cattle sacrifices and feasting undertaken during *'Id al-Adha* (the Feast of the Sacrifice).

Another, more significant, reason for the increased Hindu respect and reverence for the cow is related to the cult of

Krishna. He is the most important of the *avatars* (incarnations) of Vishnu, the preserver of the world. The pastoral aspect of Krishna depicts him as the Lord of the Herdsmen and *Govinda* ('one who brings satisfaction to the cows'), surrounded by bovines and *gopis* (cow-girls) who are devoted to him. He describes the importance of cows:

> We are cowherds, wandering in the forests, maintaining ourselves on cows, which are our wealth; cows are our deities, and mountains and forests.[13]

Probably the most compelling evidence for the sacred cow concept being alive in modern India is the continued existence of *pinjrapoles* (homes for old animals) and *goshalas* (refuges for cattle), where a few fortunate cows end their days. These animal shelters are totally uneconomical to run, because the costs of upkeep far exceed any income derived from the dung, hides and carcasses of the cows; yet they still exist. And it is still deemed political suicide to suggest that all useless or injured cows should be slaughtered in an attempt to feed the many starving people in India, as Indira Gandhi related in 1975: 'There exists no politician in India daring enough to attempt to explain to the masses that cows can be eaten.'[14]

But, ironically, there is plenty of cow suffering as a consequence of this policy, as the urban cow population is overwhelming. In Delhi, most of the estimated 40,000 cows live openly among the estimated 13 million residents. Most of these cows are left to wander freely, scavenging for food and water, and blocking up the city's roads. Many of them are neglected, ill-fed and riddled with disease. City officials employ 'urban cowboys' to round up and ship ownerless or useless animals from the suburbs out to reserves.[15]

The Festival of Cattle, Rajasthan, c. 1830, gouache on cloth. This temple wall-hanging shows Sri Nathji (a Deity of Krishna) surrounded by cows and cow-herds, as a reference to Krishna's early playground, called Golaka or 'cow-place'.

Modern travel accounts of India always contain a mention of the sacred cow and the reverence in which they are held. But, as the following extract from Norman Lewis's *A Goddess in the Stones* (1991) shows, there exists a different reality for the urban cow and the country cow:

Suddenly we were in cow-country, of the kind I had never seen before. Cities like Patna were full of cows which had to fend for themselves. They fed exclusively on rubbish and were in consequence stunted and skeletal versions of the species. In the country, however spartan the condi-

The consequence of too many city-living cattle in Kathmandu, Nepal. It is illegal to slaughter cows in Nepal, but beef can be eaten (it is imported from Christian/Moslem India).

tions, things were quite different . . . This became very apparent in an unnamed village past Bahr where we overtook a stately perambulation of thin, upright men escorting a magnificent and immaculate cow – on its way possibly to preside at some festival – which was being most carefully groomed as it plodded along by two attendant boys, one on each side. Children were running ahead flying blue kites.[16]

COW PERSONALITY: LITERARY REPRESENTATIONS

Where cows and humans have a close physical relationship (in terms of living and working side by side), they often develop an emotional bond as well, which normally results in the animals being given a name and being treated as part of the family. This close contact also allows the owner to observe the cow's personality. For those of us not lucky enough to 'know' cows, several writers have tried their best to reveal her ways.

'Cowpeaceably' is an adjective specifically created by Sterchi to describe the way cows stand placidly.[17] They will normally be ruminating, staring blankly into space and looking totally at peace. Gilbert White describes this perfectly, in regard to the cow's instinct to seek out water in the heat of summer:

> . . . that instinct by which in summer all the kine, whether oxen, cows, calves, or heifers, retire constantly to the water during the hotter hours; where, being more exempt from flies, and inhaling the coolness of that element, some belly deep, and some only to mid-leg, they ruminate and solace themselves from about ten in the morning till four in the afternoon, and then return to their feeding.[18]

Obliviously peaceful: Greek bronze of a cow.

This state of total calmness when a cow appears withdrawn and preoccupied is one to which humans sometimes aspire. Even the presence of cows can soothe the most emotional characters: the loathsome Mrs Skewton in Charles Dickens's *Dombey and Son* (1867) loves cows, which to her represent the Nature she wants to be surrounded by:

> 'I am thrown away in society. Cows are my passion. What I have ever sighed for, has been to retreat to a Swiss farm, and live entirely surrounded by cows – and china . . . What I want, is frankness, confidence, less conventionality, and freer play of soul. We are so dreadfully artificial.'[19]

D. H. Lawrence wrote at length about his relationship with Susan, a black cow which he milked on a daily basis early in the morning in 1924–5 on his ranch in Taos, New Mexico. He comments on her 'cowy oblivion', her 'cow inertia', her 'cowy passivity' and her 'cowy peace';[20] and he wonders where she goes to when in her trances. But he believes there is always 'a certain untouched chaos in her',[21] which is never far away and when her peace is broken, such as when the coyotes frighten her at night, Lawrence writes that, 'there is something *roaring* in the chaos of her universe'.[22]

Her personality has another side, one which he finds less appealing: 'To me she is fractious, tiresome, and a faggot.'[23] This is because she will deliberately do things to annoy him, such as swinging her tail in his face during milking: 'So sometimes she swings it, just on purpose: and looks at me out of the black corner of her great, pure-black eye, when I yell at her.'[24] Another flash point is when she is on heat, looking out for a bull:

> Then when I call at her, and approach, she screws round her tail and flings her sharp, elastic haunch in the air with a kick and a flick, and plunges off like a buck rabbit, or like a black demon among the pine trees, her udder swinging like a chime of bells.[25]

Lawrence describes beautifully the joys and frustrations of working or living with cows. Bringing in cows from the field to be milked can be pure pleasure on warm, sunny days, but also incredibly frustrating when time is short, because cows naturally move slowly. Whether this is to do with their bulk or their obstinacy is questionable, but the phrase 'till the cows come home' is a fitting metaphor for a long period of time.

A rather bedraggled line of cows being driven in from pasture looks like a line of indolent children, or a band of slaves being herded along. The poem 'Fetching Cows' by Norman MacCaig (1910–1996) gives the rear vantage point of a drover pushing on cows. The line of cows, as in reality, is in a pecking order, which rarely deviates:

> The black one, last as usual, swings her head
> And coils a black tongue around a grass-tuft. I
> Watch her soft weight come down, her split feet spread.

In front, the others swing and slough; they roll
Their great Greek eyes and breathe out milky gusts
From muzzles black and shiny as wet coal.[26]

This extract also alludes to the beauty of the cow, particularly the young heifers. The 'Greek eyes' is probably a reference to the heifer form into which Zeus turned the goddess Io, in an attempt to hide her from his jealous wife, Hera.

Pieter Bruegel the Elder, *The Return of the Herd*, 1565, oil on wood. In the autumn villagers bring their dairy cattle down from the summer pasture in the mountains to house them in the village over the winter.

LOVE AROUND THE COWS: DAIRYMAIDS

The association of young girls and cows is deeply engrained in European ideas of rural innocence and beauty. Dairymaids were pure, homely and healthy. Well, that was the image portrayed: it was common knowledge in the eighteenth century

ways. This was Tess Durbeyfield's habit, her temple pressing the milcher's flank, her eyes fixed on the far end of the meadow with the quiet of one lost in meditation. She was milking Old Pretty thus, and the sun chancing to be on the milking-side it shone flat upon her pink-gowned form and her white curtain-bonnet, and upon her profile, rendering it keen as a cameo cut from the dun background of the cow. She did not know that Clare had followed her round, and that he sat under his cow watching her. The stillness of her head and features was remarkable: she might have been in a trance, her eyes open, yet unseeing. Nothing in the picture moved but Old Pretty's tail and Tess's pink hands, the latter so gently as to be a rhythmic pulsation only, as it they were obeying a reflex stimulus, like a beating heart.[31]

COW ART: ALIVE AND DEAD

Dairymaids and their charges were also prominent on canvas, more so than in literature. Because of its everyday occurrence, the cow became one of the most widespread images in rural genre painting – ordinary country people doing ordinary country things. Cows are shown being milked, lounging around in the fields, chomping into grass pastures, being driven along dirt tracks and knee-deep in watering pools or rivers. Generally they are shown in a herd and the dairy cow is queen. But even though cows are depicted doing normal 'cowy things', their portrayal reflected changing societal values.[32]

The genre of cattle painting developed in the mid-1600s, principally in the Netherlands. Here, dairying and cattle rearing had become the principal land use during this time because of land reclamation programmes, and in turn became a source of national income and pride. The dairy cow became an emblem

Detail from Paulus Potter, *The Bull*, 1647, oil on canvas.

of Dutch prosperity and many 'natural' cow paintings appeared.

Paulus Potter (1625–1654) was one of the first to specialize in the genre and he almost immediately created its epitome: *The Bull* (1647). Many other painters aspired to the minutiae of the bulls' and cows' coats, their wrinkles and muscle definition. However, modern anatomical studies have shown that Potter must have created the bull from drawings of several animals at different ages.[33]

Right up until the 1790s the images of cattle were mainly factual in that they represented the reality of working animals and working peasants. Then came the romanticized image of the countryside, and of the cow, which lasted well into the nineteenth century. The notable artists of the time were Verboeckhoven in Belgium, Thomas Sidney Cooper in England, Brascassat in France and Voltz in Bavaria. They painted their landscapes and cows through rose-tinted glasses; pastures were too lush and the cattle too serene.

This mainstream style continued until the mid-1850s, when a more realist objectivity gripped European painting. The cattle, and the landscapes they stood in, looked more rugged and were more natural and everyday, as influenced by the Barbizon School in France and the Hague School in Holland.

But there is a saying, attributed to Paul Klee, that the more horrible the world is, the more abstract art becomes.[34] And the cow featured in the work of several European artists who sought to escape from the modern world and return to a primitive or child-like state. *I and the Village* (1911) by the painter Marc Chagall (1887–1985), for example, is an amalgamation of recollections from his Belarusian/Russian childhood. Chagall looks nostalgically back to a world lost to him; one in which the cow and his family, or neighbours, were interdependent.

In contrast to the close relationship of humans and cow, the German artist Franz Marc (1880–1916) envisioned a world free from humans. His *Yellow Cow* (1911) is a joyous creature fully immersed in her surroundings, moving freely and playfully, with a soft dignity. The cow is a veiled representation of his wife, Maria Franck, whom Marc had recently married, with the colour yellow symbolizing femininity, sensuality and cheerfulness.[35]

Rather more macabre is the body of art whose subject is the dead cow. The flesh or meat of the cow, and the dead cow itself,

has been employed by artists to convey different meanings. The carcass in Rembrandt's *Slaughtered Ox* (1655) looks uncannily like the Crucifixion, with the flesh looking almost beautiful with its opulent, lavish red hues. This painting inspired the work of Belarusian Chaim Soutine (1893–1943), who obsessively painted beef carcasses for very personal reasons. Soutine would keep a carcass in his studio and repeatedly daubed fresh blood on it as it dried out. During this preparation time, before he started to paint, Soutine would fast. He had a difficult relationship with food, partly because of the hunger he experienced in his youth and also because he was physiologically incapable of eating meat. His *Carcass of Beef* (overleaf) gives full rein to his carnivorous desires.

Franz Marc, *Yellow Cow*, 1911, oil on canvas.

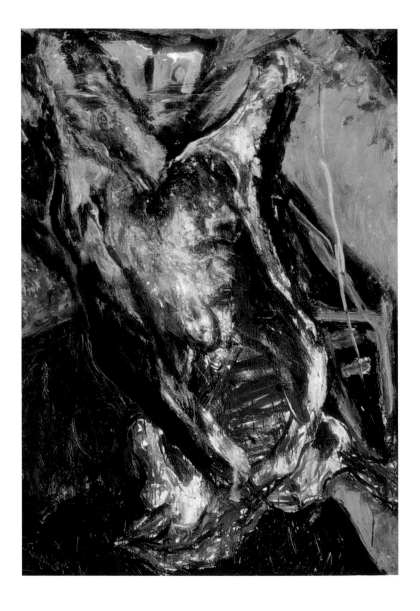

The physical appearance of meat has been used by Francis Bacon (1909–1992) as a metaphor for the horror of human pain and suffering experienced during the Second World War. Carcasses hanging in the crucifixion pose form the backdrop to his monstrous protagonist in *Painting 1946* (1946), where the carcasses retain the appearance of living flesh; human flesh and animal flesh are virtually indistinguishable.

On a more optimistic level, Damien Hirst (*b*. 1965) has used the dead cow to show the process of death as a cycle of living. Pregnant cows laterally spliced into twelve segments and displayed, out of sequence, in cabinets of formaldehyde form *Some Comfort Gained from the Acceptance of the Inherent Lies in Everything* (1996). As with Hirst's other animal works, the installation allows the viewer to really look at the physical appearance of a cow, internally and externally, and at first glance the cows also appear rather unnervingly alive.

Other cows in art include the Concrete Cows (and calves) of Milton Keynes, created in the 1960s by the American sculptor Liz Leyh. Symbolizing a lost countryside, the artist pokes fun at the preconceived notion of the 'new city', such as that voiced by the poet John Betjeman in *Slough* (1937):

Come, friendly bombs, and fall on Slough!
It isn't fit for humans now,
There isn't grass to graze a cow.
Swarm over, Death![36]

What better way to remind children growing up in Milton Keynes what cows look like? The concrete cows have led rather adventurous lives, having been kidnapped and held to ransom, placed in compromising poses, 'pyjamas' and BSE graffiti painted on them – they have even been beheaded (and then rebuilt).

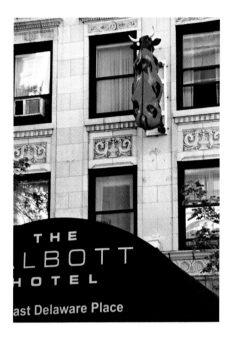

Brian Calvin, *Cowccinella Novemnotata (Nine Spotted Lady Bug Cow)*, exhibit for Cows on Parade, Chicago, 1999.

Similar eye-catching fibreglass cows have been invading and taking over major cities in the world since 1998 in the international public art exhibition CowParade. The cows are modelled on the Brown Swiss breed, after the original exhibition in Zurich, Switzerland. They are painted by artists of all ages and displayed for several months in public places, such as stations, town squares and parks. They are auctioned off at the end of the exhibition for charity. But why cows? According to the CowParade website,

Who can resist a cow? They're cute, sweet and universally beloved animals – and they're a great surprise in major urban centers. They also present a unique, three-dimen-

sional, curvy canvas for artists. See for yourself: look at
one of the cows and try not to smile.[37]

Cows are amusing; there is no denying that. But humorous cows
on television and in storybooks are portrayed as being out-of-
the-ordinary cows; different to all other cows. It is as though
cows in reality are hiding a huge secret: they are all performers,
when humans are looking the other way.

The British children's cartoon series *Blue Cow*, created by John
Olday, is one example. A blue cow lives in a field of black-and-
white cows; in every episode she gets onto a bus which stops outside her field and enjoys an adventure. When she returns in the
evening dying to tell her friends about her exciting day, they are
not interested and sigh heavily: 'She's off again.' Similarly, Cow in
the American cartoon series *Cow and Chicken* has an alter ego
called Supercow who can fly and speak Spanish. But, these are
not new phenomena: think of the nursery rhyme 'Hey diddle diddle, the cat and the fiddle / The cow jumped over the moon.'

Perhaps the most widely known comic cow is Ermintrude,
who appears in the British television series *Magic Roundabout*
and in films of the same name. Created in 1963 by Serge Danot
in the original French version *Le Manège Enchanté* as Azalée, she
brings a touch of class to her friend's drab lives, liking all classi-
cal music, architecture, singing and dance – although she is a
terrible dancer.

In contrast to the decidedly saccharine image of literary
cows (see Hardy's *Tess* above), novelist Stella Gibbons (1902–
1989) created a quartet of less attractive Jersey 'girls' in her comic
novel *Cold Comfort Farm* (1932): Graceless (whose leg happens
to fall off whilst she is being walked down a rutted lane),

Rice's Beautiful Evangeline poster c. 1896: the comic opera written by Edward E. Rice starred a dancing two-man 'heifer' acting alongside the human Evangeline.

Pointless, Feckless and Aimless. They are aged, barren and milked by an old man, Adam, who has gnarled fingers.

Other cows, real this time, in the public eye are usually Jersey cows (they have the 'ah' factor) – either advertising stars, such as Elsie the Cow (the face of the US Borden Dairy) or movie stars, such as Brown Eyes, who starred alongside Buster Keaton in the silent comedy *Go West* (1925). Keaton plays a character called Friendless and has a touching relationship with his leading lady (on and off screen). Sentimentality abounds (he ties horns to her head so that she can protect herself among the herd) and they exchange knowing looks and touches. They become inseparable, as portrayed in the film, and more literally as Keaton and Brown Eyes were physically linked together during filming by a piece of black thread.[38]

Aside from the humour, in its less endearing form, especially when used to describe a human female, the word 'cow' conjures negative images of stubbornness, arrogance, irritability and pushiness: it is a verbal insult bounded about in society by both sexes to describe women exhibiting cow-like behaviours. The derogatory description 'ugly old cow' may relate back to when the aged family cow, probably barren and therefore unproductive, would be slaughtered for its meat and hide – it was more productive dead than alive. And this is where some societies have felt discomfort about the cow, particularly Hindus: the guilt of killing a cow, who has given her all.

Over time, cows have become symbols of stupidity, low spirits, the downtrodden and agriculture – all of which are covered in the

On a street in India: even sacred oxen have bad days.

Spanish film *Vacas* ('Cows', 1992). Three generations of cows watch over the rivalries and loves of two families of Basque woodcutters. The cows just look on without judgement while the humans are forced to confront the precariousness of their rural existence.

In a similar vein, the Iranian film *Gav* ('The Cow', 1969), shows a peasant being driven to despair and finally into madness when his adored pregnant cow dies in his absence. He is left alone, and without a livelihood. The villagers lie and tell him she has disappeared, but eventually he identifies so closely with his cow that he begins to embody her in spirit and body. On a political level, *Gav*'s depiction of the futility of rural life stood in direct contrast to the propaganda for the Shah's agrarian reform policy and, at first, earned the film a government ban.

The image of the downtrodden woman, living in an urban environment, is explored in *Poor Cow* (1967), the directorial debut of the British film-maker Ken Loach. Adapted from a novel by Nell Dunn of the same name, the film tells the story of Joy (irony intended), a young girl living in 1960s London in a grim flat with her young son, Johnny. Her abusive husband is in jail for violent robbery, as is the man she loves and waits for. Her daily life is filled with grime and squalor, and while she struggles to create something better Joy inevitably chooses the wrong options. The only positive thing in her life is Johnny – much like the cow and calf, they have each other. Joy's final lyrical lines in Dunn's novel highlight society's view of her:

> To think when I was a kid I planned to conquer the world and if anyone saw me now they'd say, 'She's had a rough night, poor cow.'[39]

4 Toiling the Fields and a 'Cattle Complex'

Having looked at the cultural history of the bull and the cow, there is one more 'version' of *Bos* which has left a permanent mark on our society, and continues to do so today in developing countries. The ox, a castrated male, was not 'invented' until man began to take a second look at the aurochs they had domesticated, to see if they could be of more use while they were alive, rather than dead. By inventing the plough and the ox-cart in about 3200 BC, early Mesopotamians could harness the strength of their newly tamed cattle. The other innovation was the regular milking of the cow, possibly at a similar time.

These newly exploited qualities of cattle led to the formation of two distinct societies and subsistence systems: the plough-using agriculturalists, who cultivated marginal soils and built permanent homes, and the pastoralists, who relied on milk to provide a continuous flow of food without having to slaughter their stock (best illustrated in past and present Africa).[1]

THE PLOUGH AND THE OX

Before the plough was invented Neolithic agriculturalists used digging sticks and hoes to cultivate soils. But these implements were not ploughs as we know them today, but rather scratch tools or scrapers. Growing populations found themselves having to

Han Huang, *Wu niu tu* (The Five Oxen), Tang period, ink and colour on silk.

cultivate more marginal soils, which required tremendous work; animal power was needed and cattle were the obvious candidates.

The bull had long played a part in fertility rites, where he ploughed a ceremonial furrow or trampled grain into cultivated land. But his temperament was problematic; he was too wilful and downright dangerous to have in an open field for long periods. A more submissive animal was needed, so the bulls were castrated to calm them.

The hormonal transformation of the bull to ox is explained by Spanish veterinary surgeon, Sanz Egana:

> castration causes profound cellular changes of the pituitary gland with an influence on psychological activity; castration is practised on many animals precisely in order to make them more manageable; the ox displays a calm, tranquil and definitely peaceful temperament, lacking in aggressiveness, with slow reactions, submissive and easily scared.[2]

This two-handled plough, with a sowing funnel, was attached directly to the ox's horns, which were a symbol of fertility southern Mesopotamia, c. 2300 BC.

The ox, with all the strength of the bull, but with a docile temperament, could be trained to pull the plough and also ox-carts, which made transportation of bulky goods easier and quicker.

Although there is plenty of pictorial evidence for the use of oxen, there is little written evidence to explain how the oxen were trained to the yoke. The early Greek poet Hesiod (c. 700 BC) writes in his poem *Works and Days* that acquiring oxen is the first job for a young farmer, but there is no mention of their training, only instructions for building the plough. Hesiod states that the ideal 'horn-curved' oxen are nine-year-old males,

> . . . for their strength
> will be undiminished
> and they in full maturity, at their best to work with,
> for such a pair will not fight as they drive
> the furrow, and shatter
> the plow, thus leaving all the work done
> gone for nothing.[3]

He adds that the most auspicious day to yoke oxen is the twenty-seventh of the month.[4] Later, Virgil the cattle-farmer's son describes in his poem on the art of agriculture, *The Georgics*, the professional way of training oxen – starting from when they are calves:

Turn loose the other calves to graze as they will;
But begin at once the training of those you keep
To work the land; set them on the right road early
While youth still makes them amenable, ready to learn.
Bind a circlet of withy loose around their necks
And when they are used to this separate constraint,
Join them to one another by tying their collars,
Matching like to like, and make them walk in pairs.
First let them practise pulling unloaded wagons,
Their light tread scarcely marking the dusty ground,
Then weigh the beechen axle till it creaks and strains
As they haul the bronze shaft and the wheels ride forward.
You may feed them on grass and the willow's slender leaves
And marshy sedge, but while they are still unbroken
Gather corn in the blade for them. [5]

Reatinus Varro adds that if buying-in cattle they should be unbroken, aged between three and four years old, and preferably black in colour with wide black horns, broad foreheads, flat noses, broad chests and well furnished quarters.[6]

As with the training of oxen, humans also learnt with experience how to harness the most power from them. Early civilizations never really efficiently exploited their beasts. Generally, the ropes, which were attached to the plough, were tied directly to the oxen's horns, or to a bar attached to the horns – the horns were thought to contain the magical fertilizing powers of the lunar gods and goddesses. Around 3000 BC the advent of yokes, which oxen wore around their necks, allowed them to exert far greater draught to pull the plough or carts, by using their whole body rather than just their horns.

Different breeds of oxen were also reared to cope with different soil qualities and environments, and those of Italy, as described in Columella's *De Re Rustica* ('On Agriculture'), spread with the Romans throughout their empire:

> Campania generally produces small, white oxen, which are, however, well suited for their work and for the cultivation of their native soil. Umbria breeds huge white oxen, but it also produces red oxen, esteemed not less for their spirit than for their bodily strength. Etruria and Latium breed oxen which are thick-set but powerful as workers. The oxen bred in the Apennines are very tough and able to endure every kind of hardship but not comely to look upon.[7]

These oxen were employed throughout the year, rather than just during the sowing and harvest seasons, just as oxen are used today on subsistence farming systems. They are used for goods haulage, water-raising, logging, milling and road building and, in most cases, it would not be economically sound for India or African countries to replace their working oxen with mechanized farming.

SUBSISTENCE FARMING: AFRICA

Although oxen were used in Egypt to thresh cereals, pull ploughs and as pack animals, before the colonial period it was unusual to use oxen in the rest of Africa – the Europeans brought their technology with them.[8] From the seventeenth to the nineteenth centuries, ox carts were introduced to the ports and islands of Africa. In South Africa indigenous cattle were traded

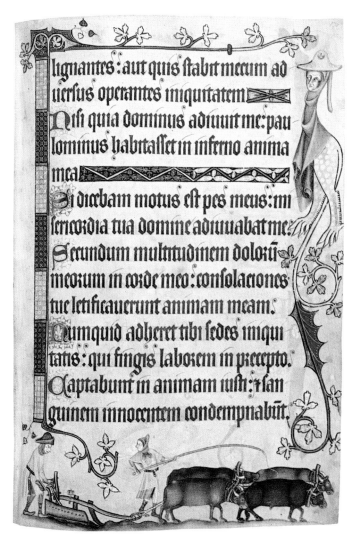

Medieval oxen trained to the plough in England: from *The Luttrell Psalter*, c. 1340.

Blinkered ox put
to work raising
water in Egypt,
c. 1908.

for Dutch goods. The settlers used the cattle to pull carts, laden
with goods and materials, to and from the ships to the settlements. Later, the semi-nomadic Dutch settlers, the *trekboers*,
travelled in four-wheeled *kakebeen* wagons pulled by at least ten
Afrikaner oxen into the hinterland of the Cape and, before the
development of the railways, all traders, miners, missionaries,
administrative and military authorities trekking through Africa
used ox-drawn wagons.

From 1900 to 1960, the colonial authorities introduced ox
labour into many sub-Saharan countries, through pilot farm
projects and training sessions for small-scale farmers. But suc-
cess was localized to areas where crops for export were grown,
and where the services of animal health care, financial aid and
training were also available.

After gaining independence, most sub-Saharan states tried
to 'tractorize' their cultivations but, because of high oil prices
and hire programmes failing, a revival of ox labour was seen

A screenshot from the film *The Big Trail* (1930) shows oxen pulling the pioneers' wagons on the Oregon Trail in the 1840s; similar to the transport used by the *trekboers* as they explored the Cape from the 1690s onwards.

Oxen employed to thresh the harvest in Palestine, c. 1900. Notice the oxen are muzzled to prevent them eating the fruits of their labour.

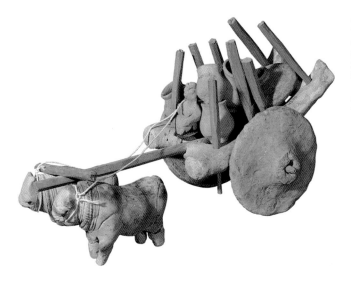

A reconstructed terracotta model of an ancient ox-cart pulled by two zebu oxen, found in Mohenjo-daro. Its design is surprisingly similar to the carts found in India and Pakistan today.

during the 1970s and 1980s via donor-supported development projects.

Today in Africa, as in medieval Europe, oxen and implements are shared between families, and the richer landowners distribute credit and employment to poorer neighbours. Cows are also increasingly taking the place of oxen, particularly in areas where oxen are in short supply, or where feed resources are stretched, making double cattle ownership impossible.

Oxen are also still widely used in India and Nepal. In these countries, where the cow is a sacred animal, and the bull is considered holy due to its association with Shiva, the zebu oxen assumes the role of the beast of burden and pulls the plough. This has been the case for millennia: rather spacious thoroughfares in the ancient Indus town at Mohenjo-daro suggest ox-carts were used, and crude terracotta models of bullock carts have been found there, dating back to about 2400 BC.

Ploughing a paddy field with oxen, Bali, Indonesia.

HARD YET PHLEGMATIC WORKER

Compared with the bull and the cow, the ox has not inspired outpourings of emotion or adulation. Being relatively androgynous, he is rather difficult to categorize. He is admired for his strength and his work ethic – the plain beast relentlessly toiling in the fields for human benefit. With his own steady gait he has plodded through history.

Accompanying the oxen is the peasant – they work so closely together that their behaviours became similar. This idea can be seen in the later writings of John Lockwood Kipling (1837–1911), the father of Rudyard, who describes the consequence of Indians working with oxen:

The lagging, measured step may compel the mind to its cadence, and the anodyne of monotony may soothe and still the temper . . . it is certain that the Indian cultivator is very like the ox . . . He is patient, and bears all that drought, flood, storm and murrain can do with the same equanimity with which the ox bears blows. When the oxen chew the cud and their masters take their nooning, the jaws of man and beast move in exactly the same manner.[9]

The work ethic of oxen puts them into a different league to other domestic animals. Their plodding nature makes them ideal draught animals in difficult conditions, particularly when breaking up soil full of tree and bush roots. For example, the New England colonists used oxen in preference to horses, because whereas the oxen would pull steadily when they met resistance in the soil, 'horses stand still, or with a start break the harness into pieces'.[10]

In the *Domesday Book* of 1086, the 'non-working' cows and bulls were rarely mentioned, compared with the plough-oxen.[11] The unit of measurement used in the *Domesday Book* was the hide, usually 120 acres, which was the amount of land that could be ploughed by a team of eight oxen in a year.[12] The *Bestiaries* (medieval illustrated descriptions of various animals) portrayed the ox as 'a strong beast that can predict the weather', this mystic ability being usually attributed to cattle in general, as they are said to lie down when rain is approaching.[13]

Similarly, Aesop uses the distinction of the heifer and the ox in one of his fables to moralize about the dangers which lie in wait for the idle. A heifer expresses her sympathy to an ox she spies at work in the fields. But, at that moment, a religious procession passes by and the ox is unyoked, but the heifer is seized by men who prepare her for sacrifice. At this sight, the ox smiles to himself and says: 'Oh, heifer, that is why you have no work to do – for you are bred to be sacrificed.'[14]

The ox was so useful to man that he was never killed for meat until he had finished his working life. Anyone who did kill an ox paid a heavy penalty (see chapter One). The Greeks even played out a ritual called the *bouphonia* or 'the ox-murder', which seemed to indicate the guilt they felt about sacrificing an ox; even if it was for Zeus, the god of sky and rain.

During the ritual, as described by James Frazer,[15] several oxen were let into a room with an altar, on which offerings had been placed – the first ox to eat these offerings thereby volunteered itself for sacrifice. After the ox was killed, its slayer was considered guilty of a crime and a trial was held to establish responsibility. All those involved in the ceremony were accused, but the actual killer had, by this time, fled. Finally, the knife that slashed the ox's throat was accused; because it could not defend itself. As its punishment it is thrown into the sea, and the hide of the ox is stuffed and yoked to a plough, to symbolize the ox's regeneration.

But despite all their hard work, and probably because of all their hard work, the ox is often described in various desultory ways. It seems that man sometimes pushed the gentle ox to the boundaries of its patience, as seen in the writings of the travel guru of the nineteenth century Sir Francis Galton (1822–1911). He describes oxen as 'coarse, gross, and phlegmatic beasts',[16] whose behaviour switches between 'sulky and ferocious'.[17] This behaviour can probably be excused when one considers that Galton used oxen as pack animals and mounts, and insists that the way to make a stubborn ox stand up was to set about 'twisting or biting his tail . . . or making a blaze with grass and a few sticks under his nostrils. The stubbornness of a half-broken ox', he adds, 'is sometimes beyond conception.'[18]

Galton also provides an insight into the extreme usefulness of the oxen for the foreign explorer. Amongst their repertoire, they acted as a life-saver in the desert, where one could slice off a piece

of flesh from the live ox, patch up the wound and continue on (the Abyssinians were seen doing this by the explorer James Bruce in 1769), or as a shield for a sportsman while stalking prey. Apparently the ox is

> said to enter into the spirit of the thing; and to show won-
> derful craft, walking round and round the object [the prey]
> in narrowing circles, and stopping to graze unconcernedly,
> on witnessing the least sign of alarm. Oxen are taught to
> obey a touch on the horn: the common but cruel way of
> training them is to hammer and batter the horns for

hours together, and on many days successively: they then become inflamed at the root and are highly sensitive.[19]

Here, briefly, we see evidence of the unpleasant and, sometimes, overtly cruel physical 'training' which oxen have been subjected to. But whereas the ox has been moulded by humans into submission, the cow has been able to retain much of her dignity as humans have had to resort to subterfuge and guile in order to get milk from her, as seen in the second society of interest in this chapter: the pastoralists, particularly those of Africa.

MILKING AND AFRICAN PASTORALISTS

Pasturalists adopt a transhumance lifestyle that involves moving their livestock – cattle in this case – between seasonal grazing areas throughout the year. The cattle are able to graze and digest the scant vegetation on marginal lands and, in turn, convert it into a protein source for humans. This is one of few ways to eke out an existence on land that receives little rainfall.

The main foodstuffs for African pastoralists are cow's milk and blood. The latter is relatively easy to collect from cattle. In Kenya and Tanzania, the Maasai shoot an arrow or dart at close range into the cow's jugular vein, then collect the spilled blood in a gourd. The blood is then either boiled to give a meat flavouring to porridge, or left to stand until it coagulates, then roasted in the embers of a fire or mixed with milk for a protein-rich meal. The cow's wound is not fatal and is patched up afterwards with clay and grasses. Ancient civilizations soon realized the main problems with cow's milk in the human diet: getting milk from the cow in the first place, and then adapting physiologically to be able to digest the lactose in raw milk.

Firstly, to get as much milk for themselves as possible they had to keep the calves away from their mothers during the day so they could not suckle all the supply (which compared to modern Western dairy cows, was meagre anyway). Then they had to collect the milk. This might seem simple, but the cow will only 'let down' her milk if a calf is present. In modern dairy milking parlours, where the calf is absent, the substitute stimulus for 'let down' is quiet handling, feeding and cleaning of the teats before attaching the milking clusters.

Pastoral peoples used, and still use, one particular method to trick cows into milking if there is no calf present; particularly if her calf has died. They will first try to deceive the cow that her calf is near her. This can be achieved by draping the dead calf's skin, scented with the calf's urine, over a person's back or an object, such as a pumpkin, or by stuffing the skin with straw. Once the cow begins to lick the fake calf she will usually 'let down' her milk. But if not, her hind legs are tied together (to stop her kicking) and then air is blown, using a special tube, into her vagina or rectum. This is done in short bursts until the

The milking of a cow, in the absence of a calf, often requires both teamwork and deception to encourage her to let go of her milk (here, the Khoikhoi of South Africa).

vagina remains fully distended with air. This induces her to stand still and 'let down' her milk.

Having collected the milk, early humans would have then realized that their digestive systems were not set up to absorb the milk-sugar, lactose, which is present in raw cow's milk. They would have experienced symptoms that would probably have put them off drinking the milk they had worked so hard to collect – diarrhoea, bloating, flatulence and stomach cramps.

But over time, with persistent drinking of raw milk, their digestive system adapted and lactose tolerance evolved in milk-drinking cultures. Pastoralists, unlike many Mediterranean peoples and the Chinese, have the ability to drink raw milk without having to turn it into butter or cheese.

CATTLE: THE BASIS OF SOCIETY

Pastoralists do not just use cattle as a source of sustenance, as seen in the travel writings of Georg Schweinfurth, who travelled in 1868 from Khartoum to Fashoda. He describes, in derogatory terms, the traditional Shilluk herdsmen whom he encountered on route:

> The men were quite naked, their lean, bony bodies plastered with the ashes . . . of cow dung, [to protect against biting insects] which gave their skins a rust-red tint . . . They wore their hair in fantastic shapes which were maintained by the repeated application of clay, gum, cow urine and dung. In consequence they smelled abominably; and since they also used cow urine for washing their milk vessels to compensate for the lack of salt, the strangers did not relish drinking with them.[20]

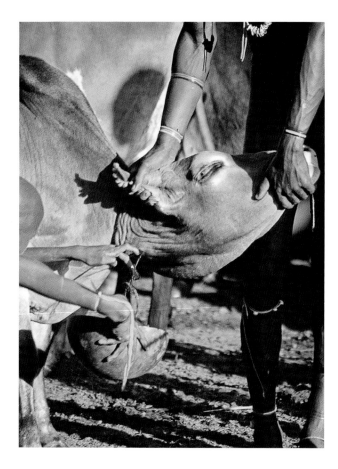

The Surma (the collective name of three pastoralist peoples in Ethiopia) collect blood from their cows, like the Maasai.

Yet there is a far deeper relationship between the African pastoralists and their cattle that goes way beyond the products of the cow. Cattle are the moveable wealth of the pastoralists and their ancestral heritage and, as such, they are treated with care and compassion. The number of cattle owned by a family, regardless of their quality, determines the family's size and their

Dinka village, southern Sudan, 1873, from G. Schweinfurth, *The Heart of Africa*. Note the men on the left burning cattle dung to ward off biting insects and that each animal is tethered by a leather collar to its own wooden peg.

social standing and/or political power in the community. Therefore, cattle accumulation is the primary goal of the pastoralists and this, traditionally, involves cattle-raiding and bloodshed between neighbouring tribes.

The Nuer of East Africa have a myth which explains why more people have died for the sake of a cow than any other cause: Man slew the mother of Cow and Buffalo. Buffalo said she would avenge her mother by attacking and killing man in the bush, while Cow said that she would remain living with man. However, she would avenge her mother by causing endless disputes about debts, bride-wealth and adultery, which would lead to fighting and deaths amongst the people.[21]

Inevitably, being this reliant on cattle, disaster can easily befall families in times of drought and cattle disease: the pastoralists' existence is a precarious one. But although cattle acquisition is all-important, even the purist pastoralists will trade or exchange their cattle with neighbouring tribes for millet, sorghum or maize during times of famine and drought, and they will sell off surplus cattle for cash to pay for school fees or taxes, or to buy other livestock.

The anthropologist Melville Herskovits (1895–1963) described the culture of the East African pastoralists as being dictated by the 'Cattle Complex'. This manifests itself in the people's strong attachment to their cattle, their love for, and identification with the animals, and a dislike of killing them, except in a ritual context.[22] Although the Eastern tribes were singled out for particular attention, it seems as though the same complex can be identified throughout Africa.

EAST AFRICAN PASTORALISTS: CATTLE AS ANCESTORS

The ownership of cattle passes through the paternal side of the family. Therefore, although children are gradually introduced through play then labour tasks to the families' cattle, it is the males who inherit. Throughout their lives they take on more and more responsibility for the cattle and their management, while the girls are generally given milking rights over certain cows.

During their cattle education, the children will learn how to describe the visual appearance of each cow in their herd. The Nuer mainly identify cattle based on their colour(s) and how these colours are distributed on the body. They recognize ten principal colours, and mixes of white and another colour can be labelled in twelve different patterns, which leads to several hundred colour permutations.

It is during their initiation that pastoralist boys symbolically begin to take over ownership of their father's cattle. The father presents his son with an ox that becomes his personal animal. This ox shapes the son's identity as he takes on a name that is linked to either the ox's coat colour and pattern, its horn shape and size, or other attributes. He will chant this ox-name as he dances before potential brides or when he takes part in sports

Pastoralist children interact with cattle through play and work.

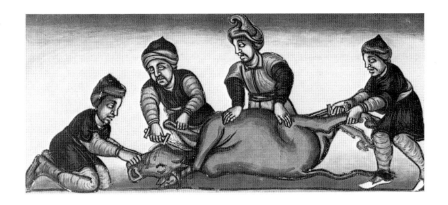

or duels and, in the past, he would have shouted the name as he hurled his spear at enemies or game.[23]

Apart from identifying with the ox, the son will also compose an ox-song which praises his beast. This is typical of pastoralist tribes, where the ownership of cattle is celebrated in song and dance. Included in these songs are references to the cattle's ancestors, and even the places where cattle graze. Cattle are represented in the dances by raised arms which resemble the large-horned animals, and in certain cases, a man will crouch on all fours, scraping his feet to raise dust, while a woman dances around him keeping a hand on his head to 'control' him.[24] These dances and songs celebrate the cattle themselves, but pastoralists are also celebrating their ancestors, nature spirits or high gods: an instance of 'cowmania' but not 'cowdolatry'.[25]

Cattle act as a vehicle for contacting ghosts and spirits because of their ownership by family lineages. The Nuer rub ash along the back of a cow or ox to get in touch with the spirit or ghost associated with it. Another way of communicating with, honouring or pleasing the ancestors and spirits is through

Ethiopians killing a 'special' cow for ritual purposes or a special feast; from an 18th-century manuscript.

the sacrifice of an oxen or barren cow (although mortuary rights require a fertile cow). The ritual of sacrifice also plays an important role in the ceremonies.[26]

When a Maasai child is born, it is immediately washed in cow-dung and the father offers a cow as sacrifice. The mother takes tail hairs from her special cow (which is given to her by her father on her marriage) and makes a necklace charm, which protects the child from evil and brings good luck.[27] On death, most pastoralist communities will slaughter a special cow from the bereaved family's herd. They wrap the deceased's body in cow-hide before burial and then partake of a funeral feast, which includes this special cow.

According to Frazer, each Dinka family possesses a sacred cow. When the country is threatened with war, famine, or any other calamity, the chiefs of the village order a particular family to surrender their sacred cow to serve as a scapegoat. The cow is driven by the women of the village (an unnatural act, as herding is done by men) to the river and across to the other bank. Here it is left to wander in the wilds and fall prey to ravening beasts. The women return to the village without looking back at the cow; if they do, they believe the ceremony will be ineffectual.[28]

The ritual killing of a white bull marks the passing of the young Maasai warriors into adulthood, during a ceremony held every five to ten years. The bull is led to a prepared area of ground and fed a numbing mix of alcoholic mead and narcotic leaves, until it becomes drowsy. Then, finally, its nostrils are stuffed with leaves and it slumps to the ground, without a hint of pain. The warriors will drink the bull's blood, mixed with mead and milk, and will be fed a piece of the cooked flesh, which they themselves cannot touch with their hands. Finally, each warrior is given a ring for his finger made from the sacrificed bull's hide.[29]

MOVEABLE WEALTH

The next rite of passage for males is to get married. But this can only happen once the family has accumulated enough cattle. The traditional form of marriage arrangement is the payment of bride-wealth to a girl's family in the form of cows. Cattle are in constant circulation between families, and each family will experience times of prosperity as their daughters marry, and times of relative poverty when their sons marry. The number of cattle for bride-wealth is negotiated between the families, and they are often paid in instalments. In most cases, the quantity of the cattle is more important than their quality.

Many groups justify the practice of exchanging girls for cattle by claiming that the wealth received compensates them for the time and trouble taken to raise a daughter – a thank-you, in effect, from the fiancé's family for bringing up their future daughter-in-law. Others view bride-wealth as compensation for

Bull-leaping by the Hamar people of the Omo Valley, Ethiopia. Young men must successfully cross the backs of the lined up cattle four times to complete their initiation, allowing them to marry, to start their own cattle herd and vote on tribal issues.

the loss of a daughter's economic services, or as payment for the children she adds to her new family.

However, the cattle handed over to the girl's family cannot be disposed of. If their daughter fails to bear children, has an affair outside of marriage or divorces, the father must return the bride-wealth. Therefore cattle determine the size of a family, as the more cattle owned the more wives can be 'bought', and the more children will be produced to help with the care of the cattle. On the other hand, a wealthy patriarch might own lots of cattle but he will not be seen as a man of importance and status unless he has extensive cattle-related social relations. For example, in Botswana the loaning of cattle is known as *mahisa*. There is no time restriction on the loan, but the owners generally get the cow's calves, while the cow can be used by the holder for milking and draught work. By loaning out cattle, the owner is minimizing the risks to his stock and in an emergency, such as theft or disease, he can call the animals back in.[30]

The ownership of cattle creates a division between rich and poor families; just as it did back in AD 1200 in the state of Great Zimbabwe. Here, the wealthy cattle owners lived on the hilltops within walls, which also enclosed their cattle kraals. The poor lived in the valleys, and herded the cattle during the day.

Another system of extreme inequality, whose history is rooted in cattle ownership, has resulted in inter-ethnic bloodshed in post-independent Rwanda. In the 1880s a military aristocracy of pastoralists developed in Rwanda where the Hutu cultivators had their chiefdoms infiltrated by Tutsi pastoralists. The minority Tutsi controlled the cattle and they distributed them to the majority Hutu farming families in return for their allegiance. The Tutsi king had the monopoly on land, cattle and royal prerogatives – the cattle were considered as evidence of, and as an emblem of, power, wealth and grace.

The Cattle of Kings or Ankole cattle, belonging to the Tutsi people, were highly prized as status symbols and played an important ceremonial role.

Under colonial rule, first by the Germans then by the Belgians, more rigid definitions of ethnicity were imposed. In the 1920s the Belgians introduced a system of identity cards specifying the tribe to which the holder belonged. A simple formula was applied to borderline cases: those with ten cows or more were Tutsi; those with fewer were Hutu.[31] This ethnic obsession grew to violent proportions when the long-oppressed majority Hutu finally took political control at independence in 1962 and retaliated against the Tutsi's past socio-economic dominance, culminating in the Rwandan genocide of April 6 to 17 July 1994 when over a million Tutsi and moderate Hutu were killed by extremist Hutu military groups.

NO CATTLE = NO SOCIETY

Disputes over cattle have been, and still are, responsible for much misery and bloodshed in Africa, particularly between the tribes living in north-west Kenya, north-east Uganda and southern Sudan: 'Cattle bring us to our enemies' is a saying of the Turkana tribe,[32] while the Nuer have a myth that the Dinka once obtained a cow by deceit, which legitimizes the Nuer's raiding of Dinka cattle.

A young Afar man from Ethiopia returns to camp after grazing his cattle in the bush all day. He wears a knife for protection against cattle raiders.

There are several reasons behind the need to raid, counter-raid and engage in outright warfare over cattle. One traditional reason is that young men regard cattle raiding as a rite of passage and as a way to acquire bride-wealth. One of the main roles of the initiated Maasai man is to be a warrior and herdsman. This means that they will defend their grazing land and cattle from raiding neighbours, and also undertake raids to gain cattle and expand their grazing. Their justification for aggressive raiding is also held in myth: their Rain god *Ngai* granted all cattle to them for safe keeping when the Earth and the Sky split.

Whatever the reason or justification, cattle raids have disrupted the lives of African tribes for centuries, but they are now more deadly thanks to the introduction of guns in the 1970s. The high mortality of both cattle and humans, and the closure of trade and medical supply routes, had led to crops being neg-

Tanzanians herding cattle into Lake Victoria for their daily drink and a cooling bath.

Piles of cattle carcasses in Niger, 2005: cattle died because of poor fodder crops due to drought and locusts, threatening the livelihoods of tribes such as the Tuareg and Fulani.

lected, subsequent food shortages, disease outbreaks and further cattle losses.[33]

Apart from cattle raiding, there are many other natural and man-made disasters which have wiped out cattle populations. Of particular note are the rinderpest (cattle plague) epidemics of 1880–90, bought to Africa by the European colonists. Rinderpest spread throughout sub-Saharan Africa, often killing 90 per cent of cattle.[34] There were severe repercussions for the pastoralists who depended on cattle, not only for their traditional ancestral worship and bride-wealth, but also their existence: many pastoralists starved.[35]

Rinderpest was not the only disaster to hit Africa in the nineteenth century: there was also smallpox, brought in from Europe, a plague of jigger flies, the wars of 'pacification' and severe droughts. The combined effect of these calamities was the obliteration of stock, harvest failures and population collapse. All of these factors resulted in bush regeneration, which produced ideal living conditions for the return and spread of the tsetse fly.

The tsetse fly is the faunal nemesis of cattle in Africa. This rather innocuous-looking fly halted the progress of cattle through the West African forest zone in the middle of the second millennium BC for about two thousand years. The tsetse sucks the cow's blood and while feeding can transmit a minute blood-parasite to its host. This parasite triggers the fatal disease known as *nagana* or cattle sickness, which ultimately causes inflammation of the brain. It was not until AD 1–200, when some cattle (the N'dama breed and the dwarf Shorthorn) eventually acquired immunity to the parasite that cattle finally reached South Africa.[36]

It was, therefore, disastrous for the pastoralists when the tsetse fly returned due to bush regeneration. It was believed in the late 1800s that game animals acted as vectors for *nagana* and also the human form of the disease – the equally deadly sleeping sickness or *trypanosomiasis*.

Although black Africans were succumbing to the latter, it was not until the Europeans' cattle came down with *nagana* that the colonists began to investigate the disease and what action they should take. In 1911 a commission led by Sir David Bruce concluded, arguably wrongly, that all large game, particularly antelope, should be culled to stop the spread of tsetse. From the 1920s through to the 1960s this was done, albeit in a rather indiscriminate way.

It was only in Southern Rhodesia, where there were large and influential settlements of white farmers whose cattle were threatened, that the culling policy appeared to succeed. From 1948 to 1951 the 987 African hunters employed managed to kill

102,025 head of game – to the rage of the preservationists who battled against the extermination.[37]

Cattle, it seems, have caused all kinds of trouble for Africans and African wildlife. But whatever the cause of cattle death it is the reliance on cattle which puts pastoral societies in most peril, wherever they are on the globe. For example, the nomadic herders of Inner Mongolia, China, were close to starvation during the harsh winters of 1999/2000 and 2000/2001, when the *dzud* occurred. This literally means 'lack of grazing', but is also translated as 'starvation due to fodder shortage' – the cattle cannot reach the grass which is sheathed in a film of ice. The Red Cross estimated that the 2000/2001 *dzud* killed 220,000 cattle and caused the deaths of nearly 40 people, as they were unable to trade their cattle for food and fodder in the towns.[38]

5 Cattle Stars and Romantic Associations

In total contrast to the pastoralists who still struggle to rely on the live cow for their livelihood, Western civilizations have reverted to being reliant mainly on the dead cow – for meat and leather. While the pastoralists are still able to retain their relationships with cattle, Europe and North America have pushed cattle to the fringes of society. But in the process of severing the intimate bond with cattle, North America built a whole culture based around the Texan Longhorn, which still retains its romantic associations, and Britain became the birthplace of selective cattle breeding.

Even though these cultural legacies serve to remind us of the importance of the dead cow to Western societies, they do at least reserve cattle a place in our cultural histories.

BRITAIN: BEEF CATTLE

During the cow's millennia of servitude to British farmers, and the public, they were never glamorized or celebrated in public life or culture before the eighteenth century. In medieval and early modern England, cattle lived alongside the rural populations, providing milk, labour and eventually meat, when they were too old or exhausted to be of use.

By the beginning of the 1500s enclosure of land enabled dairying and beef fattening to become fledgling industries, and

Medieval British cattle were small and provided tough beef, because they were not slaughtered until they were old and exhausted. From *Queen Mary's Psalter*.

those who could afford the luxury of meat ideally chose beef. In fact, by the seventeenth century the English were renowned as beef-eaters. In his journals of 1698 the French traveller Henri Misson reported that

> it is common Practice, even among People of good Substance, to have a huge Piece of Roast-Beef on Sundays, of which they stuff till they can swallow no more, and eat the rest cold, without any other Victuals, the other six Days of the Week.[1]

To meet the demand for beef, particularly in London which experienced expotential population growth during the 1700s, drovers brought large herds of Scottish and Welsh cattle and cattle from northern England southwards on foot. These cattle, having lost weight on the journey, would need to be fattened up by farmers in the Midlands, East Anglia, the Home Counties

Highland cattle being driven by drovers down to the southern markets, a sketch by James Howe, sketch, c. 1830.

and the coastal marshes from Hampshire to Kent before they were sold at London's great Smithfield cattle market.

In 1732, 76,210 cattle passed through Smithfield market.[2] At this time the British cattle population was a rag-bag of assorted local types, rather than breeds as we know today. Each county, and almost each valley in those counties, had produced cattle ideally adapted to local conditions and requirements. The breeder and farmer George Culley described in his *Observations on Livestock* (1786) the kind of cattle most prized: 'large, long-

Smithfield Market, London, 1811: the destination of many British beef cattle.

Before improvement: British cattle 'reproduced' by James Lambert in his *Countryman's Treasure*, 1683.

bodied, big-boned, coarse, gummy, flat-sided . . . and often lyery or black-fleshed'.[3] The problem was that there was just not enough meat on these animals to feed the growing, more affluent population; neither was there enough fat on them to produce the necessary quantities of tallow, which was used to light urban homes. The only way to meet demand was to improve the quality of the national herd, which had to begin with superior breeding animals.

These cattle had to grow quickly, on the least amount of food, and produce a carcass that contained as much usable flesh and fat as possible. And these qualities they had to pass on to their offspring.

It was a task for the professional breeders, led by the Leicestershire tenant farmer Robert Bakewell, affectionately known as the 'father of animal breeding'. From the 1750s, Bakewell had taken traditional white-backed, long-horned animals and selectively in-bred for characteristics he required – 'all is useless that is not beef' was one of his sayings.[4] He demonstrated that animals of close relationship could be mated, and if rigid culling was practiced, desirable characteristics could be fixed much more rapidly than by mating unrelated animals.

By the 1780s, Bakewell had created the Improved Longhorn or New Leicester cattle breed, which according to Culley was

... clean-boned, round, short-carcassed, kindly-looking and inclined to be fat; and it is a fact, that these will both eat less food in proportion, and make themselves sooner fat than the others . . .[5]

'The Fat Long-Horned Ox, bred at Dishley Farm by Honeyborn, successor of Robert Bakewell': etching by George Garrard, an artist who made small plaster models of the main cattle breeds, which were later displayed in London's Natural History Museum.

Bakewell's foundation bulls were then hired out to ordinary farmers so they also could improve their herds. Once the basics of selective breeding were established, it was not long before the breeding of cattle became a fashionable hobby among aristocratic landowners. They had the time, space and money to lavish upon their cattle.

The fact that 'men of the highest rank and fortune' had become interested in 'rural concerns' was 'nationally advantageous and conducive to the happiness of thousands', wrote the Revd Arthur Young in his *General View of the Agriculture of the County of Sussex* (1813). He added that as a consequence of Bakewell's 'extraordinary exertions', the whole country was 'electrified' with a desire to improve the genetic merit of cattle.[6]

But, not everyone was as enthusiastic as Young. Some were concerned that the purity of the breeds would be compromised, and others voiced concerns that breeders would care more

about the appearance of their cattle, over the animal's economic performance and productivity.

PATRIOTIC BEEF

The wealthy landowners claimed they were breeding improved cattle so that England could be self-sufficient in beef – it was their patriotic duty. Beef, as previously mentioned, was a luxury food that the English were very fond of. But in a time when England was threatened with foreign invasion and, in turn, with foreign attitudes and ideals, the English particularly took beef to their hearts. Beef came to have social and cultural connotations; it became a patriotic symbol.[7]

Ironically, although the word beef comes from the Old French *boef* or ox, the main target of English beef patriotism were the French, who were threatening to invade Britain during the Revolutionary and Napoleonic Wars (1792–1815).

It was a popular belief that the red meat fed to the British forces (salted beef was a staple) produced strong fighters, who could easily defeat puny, snivelling Frenchmen fed on Continental fare. The first stanza of the patriotic ballad *The Roast Beef of Old England* (originally written by Henry Fielding, but reworked and adapted many times) makes reference to this belief:

When mighty roast beef was the Englishman's food,
It ennobled our hears, and enriched our blood,
Our soldiers were brave,
Our courtiers were good
Oh the roast beef of England
And old England's roast beef!

Beef was also linked with the honest and hard-working yeoman class of English society, through the allegorical character of John Bull. He was employed by the political satirists of the day to represent the British people who were at the mercy of those abroad, as well as their own government. John Bull was often portrayed gorging himself on roast beef and those other quintessential British foods – plum pudding and ale.

CATTLE STARS

So with the pride of Britain at stake, the wealthy landowners set about changing the make-up of the national herd and creating cattle celebrities. Bakewell's Longhorns were soon superseded by the dual-purpose (providing milk and meat), roan-coloured Shorthorns, which evolved from the Teeswater and Durham cattle. The latter were improved by the farming Colling brothers, Robert and Charles. They established their herd in 1783 with

The famous
'Durham Ox',
born in 1796, was
a much-travelled
animal, and his
portrait adorned
many drawing-
room walls. He
had three owners;
the last, Mr John
Day, was offered
£2,000 for him
in 1801: the offer
was refused.

four cows – Duchess, Cherry, Strawberry, and Old Favourite – and a bull called Hubback.[8]

One of the herd's offspring was the super-sized superstar 'The Durham Ox', who toured throughout England and Scotland for over six years in a specially designed carriage, pulled by four or six horses. He was advertised as standing 5 ft 6 inches tall and weighing 3,210 lbs (1456 kg). He, and another Colling-reared monster, 'The White Heifer Who Traveled', did much for the advertising of the newly founded breed. So much so, that when the Collings' herd of Shorthorns were finally dispersed in 1810, the cattle fetched outrageously high prices. The best bull, Comet, was the first bull ever to fetch 1,000 guineas, while the best cow, Lily, fetched 410 guineas.

Many other breeds were improved and championed by certain families, such as Francis Quartly and his family, who worked on the Devon draught and beef animals. By the end of the nineteenth century, the Devon was second only in number to the Shorthorn. The breed was further improved by Thomas Coke (1754–1842) at his estate at Holkham in Norfolk: his Devons were considered to have reached breed perfection.

The improvers of each breed clubbed together to form breed societies. Their job was to promote the breed and to register the births and ancestry of all pedigree cattle to maintain the purity, and foster the improvement, of the breed. Several of the societies enjoyed royal patronage, such as the Hereford Herd Book Society, whose patron from 1878 was Queen Victoria.

The different breed societies worked together under the umbrella of local and national agricultural societies, of which there were at least 32 by 1803. These were established to promote the most profitable cattle and sheep breeds to the ordinary farmers. Each society held an annual show, but the first to do this was the Smithfield Club in London, which organized a Christmas exhibition in 1799. This event, known as the Smithfield Club Cattle Show, was the wider farming public's first glimpse of the new breed improvements. For the breeders themselves, it was an opportunity to establish quality standards and compare each other's breeding achievements. The event became a longstanding highlight of the London social calendar, being visited by the nobility and the royal family, but was also *the* highlight of the ordinary farmers' year.

Until the mid-1800s the show cattle were cruelly fattened to gargantuan sizes, such as the Great Herefordshire Ox, who stood at 6 ft 4 inches high, was 10 ft round and weighed 5,140 lbs (2,331 kg). Butchers queued up at the end of Smithfield Shows to buy the carcasses of the prize-winning cattle. The public would then gawp at the extremely fatty cuts displayed in the butchers' windows, and wealthy customers would pay over the odds to buy the meat. They could then impress their guests at Christmas by giving the show name of the roast beef set before them.

However, it can only be guessed what response the following extract from the *Quarterly Review of Agriculture* (1835–6)

would have got from ordinary farmers sitting around their kitchen tables. Shorthorns were described as

> Irresistibly attractive . . . the exquisitely symmetrical form of the body . . . bedecked with the skin of the richest hues . . . ornamented with a small . . . head [and] prominent mildly beaming eyes.[9]

This glorification of the aesthetics of the animal seems to suggest that the original impetus to improve British cattle had got lost amongst the wealthy landowners' need for a societal hobby. The result was grossly overweight cattle, whose spindly legs could hardly hold up their gigantic bodies, and who suffered from infertility and susceptibility to disease.[10]

The proud owners of pedigree cattle often asked artists to add on more flesh and height to their animal's portrait: J. H. Carter, *Sir Charles Morgan, Bt, Presenting his Prize Bull to King William IV*, painted in the 1830s.

The owners were so proud of their animals that they brought in artists to record their creations for posterity, encouraging the artists to exaggerate muscle and fat reserves. The famous engraver Thomas Bewick (1753–1828) wrote that when he was a young artist there had been a

> rage for fat cattle, fed up to so great a weight and bulk as it was possible for feeding to make them; but this was not enough; they were to be figured monstrously fat before the owners of them could be pleased.[11]

The recording of bloodlines also became an obsession for breeders: just as their own ancestry was recorded in *Debrett's Peerage and Baronetage*. They recorded the parentage of each of their animals and the most importance consideration was 'the length of time there had been a succession of best blood, without any inferior blood intervening'.[12] Eventually, George Coats produced the first detailed list of every pedigree Shorthorn going back to 1734 in the *General Short-Horned Herd Book* (1822). It contained the records of 710 bulls and 850 cows – many of whose genetics would later be used in the foundation of 40 different breeds worldwide, such as the American Santa Gertudis and the Australian Droughtmaster.

After this publication, which became as popular as the Bible on many farmhouse tables, each championed breed gained a herd book. Rumours of inaccurate pedigrees in 1874 incited Shorthorn breeders to form the Shorthorn Society, which was the first breed society of its kind, and this organization took over the herd book.

Despite the pomp and ceremony surrounding these pedigree animals, their genetics were, in time, spread throughout the commercial cattle of Britain. And, in Scotland, the Scottish Highland, Galloway and Aberdeen Angus breeds gained reputations for producing beef to match their southern counterparts.

By 1830, the numbers of cattle going through Smithfield per year had increased to 159,907,[13] and they were larger and heavier. The domestic and global beef industries were assured, thanks to the genetics of the beef-stars.

But, while selective breeding of cattle, and its advantages, were being celebrated and put into good use in Britain, the fledgling Texan beef industry in America was concentrating on their wiry and lean Longhorn cattle. It was not until the 1880s that the improved British breeds really began to make an impact in North America.

US CATTLE: THE FINAL GREAT CATTLE CULTURE

It was not only a beef industry that grew up around the Texan Longhorns, but also a culture. Their ancestors were the Spanish

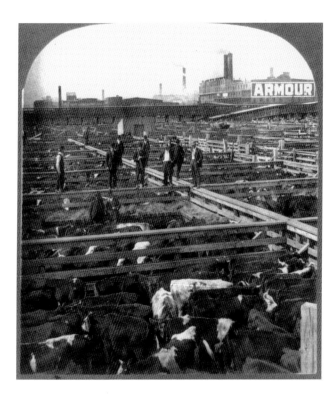

The centre of the American cattle boom during the 1860s and 1870s: the Union Stockyard in Chicago.

Criollo type, which had themselves evolved from the Iberian Peninsula cattle originally imported into mainland America by the Spanish conquistadors in the early 1500s.

These Longhorns were wiry, tough, aggressive and resilient.[14] However, as with the unimproved cattle of Britain, there was very little meat on them. Butchers derided the Longhorn as 'eight pounds of hamburger on 800 pounds of bone and horn'.[15] However, these semi-wild cattle living in huge numbers on the coastal plains of Texas were to become the 'stars' of American's open range cattle industry – an industry which, in fact, only lasted for twenty years, but which has, and will, last in legend for many more.

In the 1830s, although the Longhorn cattle outnumbered Texans by six to one, there was no real beef industry; only a trade in hides and tallow for candles, which meant carcasses were left to rot where cattle had been slaughtered. The cattle belonged to whoever cared to claim them. In the 1850s some cattle were driven outside Texas to supply fresh beef for prospectors during the Californian Gold Rush, to New Orleans and Chicago, and in 1854 the first Longhorns arrived in New York. However, these early movements of cattle were perilous and time-consuming for the ranchers and, much to the outrage of other states, the Texan cattle spread fatal tick fever to cattle en route (Texan cattle were immune to the ticks they carried). The resulting quarantine laws banned the passage of Texan cattle northwards, and the Civil War of 1861–65 temporarily halted the Longhorns' progress anywhere.

When the Texan ranchers returned home after the Civil War, they found five million head of cattle roaming freely, unbranded and worthless, without a paying market. They paid little or no attention to their herds, until the railroads extended westwards in the form of the Union Pacific Eastern Division (begun in 1863 and later renamed as the Kansas Pacific Railroad). This rail link allowed them to export their worthless cattle, via the Union Stockyard in Chicago, to the burgeoning and lucrative markets in the north-east, and to the east where immigrants were arriving from Europe. The stockyards of Chicago opened in 1865 and covered a 345-acre site where nine railroads converged. At its peak, the yards were capable of handling 21,000 cattle a day and Chicago became known as 'The Great Bovine City of the World'.[16]

It was easy for the Texan ranchers to create a herd of Longhorns. Most just found themselves a watering place on their range, adopted a brand and hunted down all the 'maver-icks' (unbranded cattle) within the area and claimed them.

THE LONG DRIVE

The days of the cattle drive, or 'long drive' began in earnest in 1867 when Texan cattle were driven along the Chisholm Trail, which snaked through Texas and into Kansas, to the railhead at Abilene. It was here that the enterprising Joseph G. McCoy had built the first 'cattle town' the previous year, where southern drovers and northern buyers could meet and, importantly, the Texan ticks were killed off following the hard winter frosts.

During the summer of 1867, an estimated 35,000 cattle came up the Chisholm Trail, were fattened over the winter on the grassy, well-watered plains surrounding Abilene, and then sent, tick-free, eastward by rail in open pens. Over the next twenty years the cow towns had to move further west to accommodate the westerly movement of farmers who lobbied against the damage caused to their crops by the 'tick-ridden' Texan cattle.

The first representation of a cattle drive in an American magazine: *A Drove of Texas Cattle Crossing a Stream*; wood-engraving after A. R. Ward, in *Harper's Weekly*, 19 October 1867.

Abilene and the subsequent Kansas cattle towns of Ellsworth, Dodge City and Hays received in total two million Texan cattle.

In addition to the railroads, Texan cattle were also being driven further north to the Great Plains following the Goodnight-Loving Trail, named after the pioneering Texans Charles Goodnight and his partner Oliver Loving, who sold cattle to J. W. Iliff, the first of Colorado's cattle kings.

Iliff had discovered that cattle could live and thrive on the scanty-looking bunchgrass which covered the Great Plains. He began buying lame, old and ill cattle from goldseekers and travellers on the Oregon Trail. Then he, and the many ranchers who settled on this free public grass, sold their fattened cattle to the Rocky Mountain miners and the Native Indians who had been forced into government reserves.

From 1867 to 1886 there were about six to nine million Texas Longhorns driven to the railheads and the plains. The 500-mile drive to the Kansas railheads took around three months, while drives to Montana or Dakota took six months.

After over-wintering, the next journey for Longhorns in the 1860s and early 1870s was on the railroads to the Union Stock Yards in Chicago. Butchers from the north and east would gather there to buy the cattle and, before refrigeration was introduced in the 1860s, the cattle were shipped on to the east for butchering at local slaughterhouses.

CATTLE AND COWBOYS

The icons of the American West were, and still are, the cowboys who drove these cattle. The cowboy, or cowpuncher, was employed by the Texan ranchers to round up the cattle and then accompany them on the drive. They are depicted in a romantic, mythical way in countless movies and novels of the Western genre, with no regard for the real cowboys' understanding of cattle behaviour and their empathy with the cow. The best cowboys, such as trail driver Ab Blocker, knew their cows: 'he savies [*sic*] the cow – cow psychology, cow anatomy, cow dietetics – cow nature in general and cow nature in particular.'[17]

The persistent image is of a white, rugged, spotlessly attired, free and independent, gun-slinging man, who fights marauding Indians and cattle rustlers, and when required, rescues maidens in distress along the way. Filmmakers and novelists of the American West have, in the main, neglected the actual cattle, even though they were the reason for the cowboy's existence. Few film posters feature cattle, and Owen Wister's cowboy *The Virginian* (1902) has been labelled 'the cowboy without cattle'.[18]

Cattle rarely get any poster space on Western film advertising. Even the video cover for the first episode of TV series *Rawhide* makes do with painted Longhorns.

Those cowboys literate enough have tried to redress the balance by showing the public a very different lifestyle, such as Andy Adams, whose fictional memoirs *The Log of a Cowboy: A Narrative of the Old Trail Days* (1903) records a distinctly unglamorous, dangerous and exhausting life. Cowboys were generally young Southerners, blacks, Mexicans and Indians: they were mainly cheap, itinerant labour, and their dress, language and equipment were all borrowed from the Mexican *vaqueros* who trailed after the freely roaming Criollos.

The first spring roundup or 'rodeo' saw all the cattle gathered up from around the ranges. Over an area of 4,000 square miles, this may involve finding 10,000 cattle, which could take up to three months. The cowboys would be sent out in different directions around a central point and would return, slowly and patiently, herding the cattle and calves they found, which were sometimes stuck in bogs or hiding in bushes. From the collected herd, the best were selected for market, while immature animals were 'cut out' and returned to the range. The cowboys performed other tasks at this time, such as dehorning if the horns

Branding the mavericks: each cattle ranch had (and still has) its own brand mark, which was used to claim, or identify, unmarked cattle or calves.

were too long or too sharp, branding mavericks with the owner's mark and castrating the male calves.

After the spring round-up, around two-thirds of the cowboys would be laid off; the favoured few would be retained on the ranch for odd jobs or given the task of taking the cattle to market. A trail boss and ten cowpunchers, with 100–150 horses, would accompany an average drive of 1,500 head of cattle.

At the beginning of the trail the cattle were jittery and had to be pushed briskly along to stop them breaking for home, but after a few days they took up a natural pecking order and marched along at a good pace. They were able to cover up to fifteen miles a day. The cattle were grazed three times a day, while the cowboys had their meals. At sunset, the cattle were rounded up tightly and several cowboys would ride around them all night long, singing or whistling continuously, 'so that the sleeping herd may know that a friend and not an enemy is keeping vigil over their dreams'.[19]

On top of the short rations, choking dust, rain, mosquitoes, heat and fourteen-hour days in the saddle which the cowboys had to endure, there was also the constant risk of dangerous cattle stampedes and the risks associated with crossing the seven rivers en route to Kansas. Yet the number one enemy of the Longhorn was the heel fly, which would often cause the herd to bolt. To escape the fly, if there was water nearby the cattle would go and stand in it, or they would squat down in the brush in an attempt to cover their ankles.

The animals were also particularly susceptible to being spooked at night, and stampedes were a constant worry, especially during thunder and lightning. Rather romanticized film depictions of stampedes are found in *Red River* (1948), *Cowboy* (1958) and *City Slickers* (1991). But in reality, stampedes usually ended in grisly circumstances, such as the report of a stampede in Idaho in 1889 which killed 341 cattle, two horses and one cowboy, who was 'mangled to sausage meat'.[20] It took days, or even weeks, to round up the herd again.

During the spring, the rivers, which were usually wide, slow and muddy, became raging torrents. Several things could go wrong: cattle drives might pile up waiting to cross the swollen

" The Stampede " by Frederic Remington

Frederic Remington *The Stampede,* sculpture, c. 1910. A stampede was one of the nightmare situations facing cowboys during the cattle drive.

Cattle roaming free on the Great Plains of Montana, c. 1911.

rivers, thirst-maddened cattle could stampede, or if the leading cattle were spooked and attempted to turn around while in the river, it would cause the followers to mill around, become exhausted and drift downstream to be drowned. Occasionally the cattle could not even be persuaded to cross the rivers, as the heart-breaking diary of cowpuncher George C. Duffield shows:

> June 23: Worked all day hard in the river trying to make the beeves swim and did not get one over. Had to go back to prairie sick and discouraged. Have *not* got the *Blues* but am in *Hel of a Fix*.[21]

Unlike the movies, it was rare for the drives to be attacked by Indians or rustlers. More likely, Indians would stop the drive to

demand money for the cattle to cross their land or they would
beg for food. The trail boss would also have to deal with irate
farmers if cattle strayed on to their crops.

The boom time of the American cattle business was in the late
1870s and early 1880s – a time when American ranchers and
American and European investors joined forces to create 'cattle'
fortunes.

Investors looked to the 'free' grass on the Great Plains. This
land, which had been opened up by the mass slaughter of buffalo and subsequent removal of the Native Indians into government reserves, was there for the taking.[22] Investment in the
ranching business became a mania in America and Europe, following tales of enormous profits and guaranteed home-grown
markets (especially government contracts to feed the reserva-
tion Indians). Export markets were also booming, with every
transcontinental steamship equipped with refrigeration by
1880, which meant chilled beef could reach Britain and Europe
in perfect condition.

It was hard not to be tempted by the eulogizing of
Connecticut's Judge Sherwood, who wrote in a letter to potential backers:

> The profits are enormous. There is no business like it in the
> world, and the whole secret is, it costs nothing to feed the
> cattle. They grow without eating your money. They literally
> raise themselves.[23]

Specific examples of those who had made money in the
cattle business were cited in James S. Brisbin's pamphlet, the

plain-speaking *The Beef Bonanza, or How to Get Rich on the Plains* (1881), where annual profits of 25 per cent were regularly cited: an initial investment of $25,000 would yield a net profit of $36,500 in five years.[24] With propaganda that persuasive, it was not surprising that thousands of acres of Montana, Texas and Wyoming were bought up by cattle companies based in London and Edinburgh. From 1880 to 1885, the British and Scottish investors poured $40 million into ranching, and by then a government report stated that 1,365,000 square miles, or 44 per cent of US land, was devoted to raising cattle.[25]

During the summer of 1883 so many trail herds came up from Texas that cowpuncher 'Teddy Blue' Abbott remarked in his memoirs that 'all the cattle in the world were coming up from Texas'.[26] Over a rise near the North Platte he saw seven trails grazing behind him, eight herds ahead and across the river he could see the trail dust from thirteen other herds.

But the boom was not to last. Overstocking of the ranges, tumbling prices, range wars and blizzards all played their part in bringing the cattle bonanza to an end. However, it was the extension of the railways further west (which made it unprofitable to drive cattle up from Texas) and the erection of barbed-wire fences which killed off the Longhorn cattle culture.

BARBED WIRE

When in 1873 Illinois farmer Joseph F. Glidden patented the barbed wire which was to become the most commonly used in the American West, he had no idea of the consequences it would have on the Longhorn cattle. At first, this new technology was opposed by many large Texan ranchers, who called it the 'Devil's Rope'. They regarded it as cruel and dangerous to their cattle, and totally against the culture of open range ranching, where the Longhorns could drift uncontrolled across the range in search of water, grazing and shelter. It was during round-ups that cattle from neighbouring ranches could be sorted and driven back to their home grazing: there was no need for fencing.

However, after being convinced that the barbed wire would not harm their cattle, most north Texan ranchers made a concession and in 1881 began building fences to stop their cattle drifting further north in the winter. Their use of barbed wire escalated when new industry entrants (or 'range pirates' as the established rangers called them) started trying to claim 'free' range. The established ranchers did not want to have to buy or lease land that they felt was *theirs* by rights. So to protect their grass, cattle and wealth from being swallowed up, they used barbed wire to fence off streams and waterholes on their land. Under the 1862 Homestead Act settlers could file claims of ownership to range land by securing water rights.

It was not until the drought of 1883, when the 'pirates' realized that their traditional water points, which had always been open to all, were now enclosed. They responded by cutting the fences – and the notorious 'barbed wire wars' ensued. The disputes between the cattle barons and the incomers grew increasingly bitter and soon violence erupted amid accusations of cattle rustling, leaving three people dead.

THE END OF THE LONGHORNS

Although human lives were lost as a consequence of the fencing of the open range, this was nothing compared to the loss of Longhorns during the winters of 1884–5 and 1886–7: the worst recorded in the West. Cattle could not penetrate the deep snow to reach grazing, and in an attempt to drift before the storms, they piled into the barbed wire fences and died in their thousands, frozen and starving.

In Wyoming, one rancher recovered only 100 cattle from a herd of 5,500 head that he had turned on to the range in the autumn. The Montana rancher Granville Stuart was heartbroken by the sight of the suffering of the dead and dying cattle on his ranges, and swore never again to own an animal that he could not feed and shelter. This meant ranchers had to fence their land, restrict the head of cattle they owned and provide winter feed for them.[27]

The era of long drives, cowboys and open range ranching was over. Many ranchers went bust and by 1887 5,000–7,000 head of cattle were arriving every day for sale in Chicago.

The days of Longhorn domination were also over. As the surviving ranchers reorganized themselves, they took advantage of the improved breeds of British cattle that were being imported into Texas by the thousand. The Shorthorn, Aberdeen Angus and Devon breeds were experimented with first, but it was the Hereford that became the Longhorn's successor. As well as being able to survive the rough ranching conditions, the Herefords grew faster and produced higher beef yields – there was more

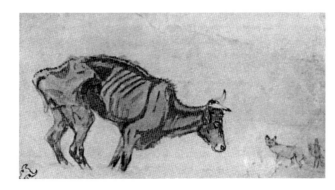

Charles M. Russell, *Waiting for a Chinook*, 1886: Longhorns had their numbers drastically reduced by the harsh winter weather.

Albert the Hereford Bull stands in Audubon, Iowa, as a monument to the national beef industry: he is claimed to be the largest bull in the world, weighing in at 45 tonnes and standing over 9 metres high.

profit in Herefords than in the 'scrub cattle'. In 1880 200 head were imported, but in the following nine years, 3,500 head were sent to the United States.

Soon the Longhorns became an endangered species, and by the 1920s only a few small herds remained. Luckily, in 1927 the Forest Service stepped in and established a herd in the Wichita Mountains Wildlife Refuge, Oklahoma, which grew to several hundred head. The Longhorn is also once again established in Texas.[28]

SOUTH AMERICA AND AUSTRALIA

With the collapse of the cattle market in North America, cattle investors looked south to Argentina for their next business opportunity. They took over the abattoirs and freezing plants (*frigorificos*) that lined the rivers Plate and Parana in the early 1900s, supplying chilled beef to Europe. By this time the beef industry was booming, with cattle being reared inland on

Cattle and *huasos* (Chilean cowboys) after a round-up, a photo taken sometime between 1890 and 1923.

extensive ranches (*estancias*), and then transported by rail to the factories.[29]

The Argentine industry had come a long way from very humble beginnings. Coming in the wake of Spanish colonists, in 1552 initial imports of Spanish Criollo cattle to the country numbered only seven cows and one bull.[30] As the colonies grew a further 4,000 head of cattle were imported to provided all the hides and meat required. However, the ideal conditions on the Pampas plains of Argentina meant that cattle thrived. By about 1615, surplus hides were being sold to Spain and Brazil, and a large salting works was built at Buenos Aires in 1717 to take advantage of the export market for salted beef, which complemented jerked (dried) beef production.

As occurred in North America, the native cattle had to be genetically improved to meet demand. In 1865 the first Shorthorn cattle arrived and the formation of the Argentine Rural Society soon followed, aiming to develop a well-organized cattle industry. Shipments of live cattle arrived in Britain from Argentina, where they were disembarked and slaughtered near London at Deptford on the south bank of the River Thames; over one million head of cattle were imported by 1879. But this industry was fairly short-lived as in 1900 an embargo was placed on Argentine cattle for three years after they brought foot-and-mouth disease into the country. An alternative to live exports had to be found, and the solution was chilled beef.

Early investors had seen the potential of refrigeration to open up export markets, as witnessed at Campana on the River Parana, where The River Plate Fresh Meat Co. built a freezing works in 1882. But by 1901 technological advances allowed chilled rather than frozen beef to be shipped across to Britain within three weeks. The ranch owners, with no live export market, had the opportunity to supply their best quality beef to this chilled market, while lower grade meat was frozen.

The South American cattle culture is no longer concentrated in Argentina, but in Brazil (see next chapter), where there are 36.5 million beef cattle, compared with 14.4 million of them in Argentina.[31]

Australia is the other major exporter of beef cattle today (with 8.8 million beef cattle), but the beginnings of its industry were even more inauspicious than that of Argentina. Along with the first shipment of 737 English convicts to Port Jackson, New South Wales, on 26 January 1788 came two Afrikaner bulls and five cows, which had been purchased en route in Cape Town. Of these cattle, the prize-bull Gorgon and four of the five cows strayed into the scrub and were lost in August of the same year.[32] They were

Brahman bull: specially bred in America from four different Indian zebu breeds, the Brahman was imported into Australia in large numbers in 1933. Since then, Brahman genetics are said to be in over 50 per cent of Australian cattle and the breed is credited with saving the Australian cattle industry from collapse, as they are able to tolerate the Northern humid tropical conditions, as well as thriving in dry sub-tropical areas.

eventually found again in 1795 (completely feral), having travelled 70 kilometres in a south-westerly direction to find tastier grazing, settling in an area later known as 'Cow Pastures'. By this time their numbers had grown to sixty-one.

Initially, the colonists had great difficulty coping with the extremes of the Australian climate, especially the droughts. It was not until better grazing was found inland that sheep-raising, and subsequently cattle-raising, became tenable. The cattle population was later boosted by imports of Shorthorns in 1825, and a year later by imported Herefords.

To meet the British demand for beef, the colony of Australia pioneered the production of tinned beef, as featured in the Great Exhibition of 1851. The product was mostly used as ship rations, but then reached the English market in 1867 as corned beef. The real breakthrough for the Australian beef industry came in 1880 when 40 tons of frozen beef were successfully shipped to London on the *Strathleven*, leading to the establishment of an export industry, which was worth more than £1m by 1890 (also including mutton exports).[33] These markets acted as a catalyst for larger-scale cattle stations to be established in the north of the country, especially in Queensland, which became, and still is, the main 'beef state'.

6 Poor Cow: Pushing the Boundaries

So far, we have seen how humans have progressively harnessed the natural abilities of cattle to provide enough meat, milk and power to meet demand. But in the West, and in the emerging economies in the Far East, we have now entered into a new era in the history of cow/human relations, where mass production has demeaned cattle to objects, with little or no human contact.

While beef cattle are still reared on the grass ranges of North America, they are usually destined to end up in beef-lots, where they are fattened on cereals before slaughter. The American consumer market now demands more tender and, therefore, fattier beef than the grass-fed Longhorns could ever produce. As such, the production of beef has had to change, using technology and science to push cattle beyond their natural abilities. The dairy cow has been subjected to the same exploitation.

However, humans are finding to their cost that there are consequences to this forced, unnatural production in terms of public health and environmental damage, and the negative effects on cattle welfare are pricking the global conscience.

UNNATURAL PRODUCTION

Product advertising bombards us with images of laughing, dancing cows, relaxing in the sun, willingly giving us control

Хороши мои красавицы-всем на выставке понравятся!

over their bodies. But all of these portraits hide the truth of intensive milk, beef and veal production. The Canadian documentary-maker Jennifer Abbott recently juxtaposed product advertising with the reality of production and slaughter in *A Cow at My Table* (1998). Screen shots of meat industry promotions show a cow wearing sunglasses, leaning back on a haystack with one 'arm' behind her head, while feeding herself hay with the other, and a smiling cow sitting upright in the back of a pickup truck on its way to slaughter.

The public should know how cattle are raised, because with the advances of technology and science, many everyday items are made from the cow, ranging from household goods to industrial products and pharmaceuticals. While 54 per cent of a slaughtered cow is used as beef products for human and pet consumption, the rest of the carcass (fat, bones, viscera and hide) is broken

Mid-1950s Soviet poster promoting the cattle industry: the dairy cow contentedly providing humanity with her milk . . . ?

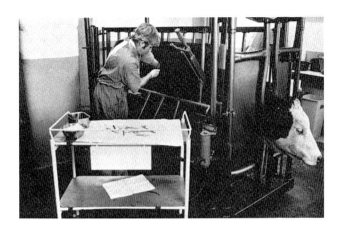

Embryos from a pedigree cow can be transplanted into a number of carrier cows, who act as surrogate mothers to 'supercow' calves.

down by renderers into a range of other substances. For example, beef fat and fatty acids are used in shoe creams, crayons, floor wax, margarine, cosmetics, deodorants, detergents, soaps, perfumes, insecticides, linoleum, insulation and refrigerants.[1]

Viewed as a set of end products, the cow loses all of its individuality and personality. It is easy to understand how the executives of fast-food companies and the supermarkets dictate to cattle farmers what 'animal units' they require for their product ranges. And while it would be relatively easy to find out how beef and milk are produced by looking at the farming press and Internet sites, how many people feel compelled to do so?

Several key points highlight the extreme demands now placed on many dairy cattle, especially in America, where the population of just over nine million dairy cows produce 80.2 million tonnes of milk annually.[2]

In what could be considered as another step forward in the domestication of cattle, the artificial insemination method is used to breed genetically superior production cows and bulls to create 'supercows' for achieving high milk yields. Production figures for Britain show that average milk yields have risen continuously, while the number of cows has fallen. In 1970 a cow produced an average of 3,750 litres (6,600 pints) of milk every year; in 1998 this figure was 5,790 litres and for the 2005/6 production year the milk yields increased to 6,787 litres (over 10,000 pints) a year.[3]

But while Robert Bakewell might look on with awe and pride at the advances in genetic selection, there are many who feel the cow's future is being put at risk. The geneticist Steve Jones argues that the reliance on a small number of bulls from a few breeds to sire the world's cows has meant that the genes of 'untold others have been lost'. Jones cites a Dutch bull called Sunny Boy, who died in 1997 after siring his two-millionth calf.[4] And, although the Ancients, who worshipped the bull for his fecundity and vigour, would be impressed with these figures, it leaves the cow in a precarious position if disease hits, market demands change or the environment alters drastically.

There is also a physical cost to these high milk yields – the cows have to work hard to synthesize milk from their feed

A cowhide-covered framework is used to collect a bull's semen. His semen is then destined to impregnate thousands of real cows, without any physical contact involved.

intake. The daily work rate of a cow producing a peak yield of 35 litres (61 pints) of milk each day, has been compared to a man jogging for six hours every day of the week.[5] In as little as three years, milking cows become worn out, and when their milk yields fall they are slaughtered and enter the food chain. Even though the majority of farmers work extremely hard to maintain the health of their cattle, when cows are confined in unnatural, man-made environments and rely totally on humans for their survival (particularly during winter housing or in all-year-round housing systems), there are bound to be adverse effects on these cows. The most common health problems are infertility, mastitis, lameness and metabolic disorders, caused by inadequate feeding and housing, faulty milking equipment or poor hygiene. For example, each year 25–55 per cent of dairy cattle in England and Wales experience some form of lameness and 15–20 per cent of dairy cattle have their udder infected with sub-clinical mastitis.[6] The dairy cow is also subject to a continuous cycle of calving, milking and impregnation, enabling her to lactate for about 305 days of the year. She will calve, and nearly three months later become pregnant again, so she is pregnant and milking for eight months, then she is 'dried off' (not milked) for two months before calving again.

Just as a further pressure on American milkers, their milk yields can be further boosted by at least 10–15 per cent by being injected with a genetically engineered bovine growth hormone called recombinant bovine somatotropin (rbST). Although this hormone has been commercially used in the US since 1994, its use has been banned in the EU since 1990, primarily for economic reasons, rather than welfare reasons, because the extra milk yields would upset milk prices.

While we are pushing the dairy cow to produce about ten times the amount of milk which she would normally produce for a calf, the life of an intensive beef cow is generally regarded as less harmful to the cow. Exposés of American beef-lots by campaigners and journalists tend to concentrate on the fact that the cattle live in a barren environment that is uninteresting for them, especially after living on the grass ranges.

The main issue for the general public, however, is the perceived threat to human health from producing meat under beef-lot conditions, particularly the spread of *E. coli 0157:7*. Eric Schlosser's exposé of the ways modern beef production meets the demands of the fast-food consumer caused uproar in 2001 when the book *Fast Food Nation* was first published (subsequently repackaged and republished for the teenage market in 2006 as *Chew on This*).

He visits two enormous beef-lots at Greeley, Colorado, which are owned by ConAgra Beef Company, one of the major suppliers to fast-food companies. Each feed-lot can accommodate 100,000 cattle. The cows are 'crowded so closely together that it looks like a sea of cattle, a mooing, moving mass of brown and white fur that goes on for acres'.[7]

Feed-lots are essentially fenced concrete standings with feeding troughs running along the length of one side, into which their fattening diet of grains and other by-products are mechanically delivered. The cattle have come from the ranges into this unnatural environment, where they are crowded and unable to have proper exercise. Schlosser describes them as standing in pools of mud and manure, which often gets into the feed and water supplies.

The Toronto-based food writer and restaurant critic Gina

One of the 'shittiest' places in America: The stench from the packed beef-lots on the road between Bovina and Hereford, Texas, is totally overpowering.

Mallet adds to the list of horrors which can enter into the beef cattle's diet:

Cattle are given antibiotics against disease and to spur growth; and they are bulked up with an FDA-approved [US Food and Drug Administration] protein mix of restaurant leftovers, out-of-date pet food and chicken litter. Spray-dried cows' and pigs' blood is mixed into the cattle's drinking water.[8]

It's enough to put anyone off eating beef burgers . . . or is it? These concerns about the safety of eating processed beef are nothing new. A former slaughterhouse employee was quoted in

162

1898, saying that he had seen 'thousands of sick, lame, aged, and repulsive-looking animals driven in for slaughter . . . such beef was boiled and canned as corned beef'.[9]

But there is mounting pressure on the American cattle industry to instigate a complete ban on feeding cattle animal by-products, mainly as a result of the appearance of bovine spongiform encephalopathy (BSE) – the same disease which in 1996 stopped British beef exports in their tracks.

The cause of the disease outbreak in Britain was traced to a meat-and-bonemeal compound, made out of unsaleable sheep carcasses, which was being fed to cattle as a cheap source of protein. Unknown to farmers, the process to render these carcasses was changed in 1982, due to cost-cutting.[10] This allowed abnormal or infectious proteins (prions) to survive in the feed, and once inside the cow they set off a chain

Cattle were incinerated in 1996 in an effort to remove any potential risk of BSE entering the human food chain, after the first cases of vCJD came to the public's attention.

reaction that transformed native proteins into harmful ones, which multiplied and clogged up the brain: the 'Mad Cow' had arrived.

BSE was first identified in cattle in 1986 and within two years over a thousand cases were reported in over 200 herds. By 1996, official figures suggested a total of 168,317 cases of BSE had been confirmed, but in reality the total may have been over 700,000 sick cattle within the UK.[11] Conspiracy theorists have claimed that the government wanted to cover up the real number of sick cattle because in 1996 it became obvious that humans were becoming sick and dying from eating infected beef: variant Creutzfeldt Jakob disease (vCJD) had followed.

The public panic and outrage was enormous. The media coverage turned from the pitiful images of staggering dairy cows to the incineration of all cattle diagnosed with BSE, and those animals over 30 months old who were at risk of developing the disease.

Unfortunately for the cow, purely as a result of human intervention in their diet, they experienced their first major public relations disaster: in over a decade, vCJD has claimed 158 human lives in Britain.[12] And because of the long incubation period of vCJD, and its reported ability to be passed on through blood transfusions and surgical instruments, it is likely that humans will live with the threat of the disease long after BSE has been eradicated from cattle.

ENVIRONMENT: HOOFED LOCUSTS AND MASS POLLUTERS

Environmentalists have also demonized beef farmers and their cattle for turning virgin Latin American rainforest into 'an eroded wasteland'. The Food and Agriculture Organization (FAO) estimates that in Central America the forest area has been reduced by almost 40 per cent over the past 40 years, while pasture area

Nelore cattle pasturing on land which was once part of the Atlantic Coastal Rainforest in southeast Brazil. The cattle are waiting to be being vaccinated against foot-and-mouth disease.

has been rapidly increasing for the growing cattle population. Studies predict that, by the year 2010, cattle will be grazing on more than 24 million hectares of land that was forest in the year 2000, and that nearly two-thirds of the deforested land will be converted to pasture.[13]

Environmentalists also condemn the wasteful use of cereals being fed to beef animals when people are starving in the world, and the treatment of manure, which if not properly managed causes air, soil and water pollution.

Schlosser quotes that a typical steer consumes more than 3,000 lbs of grain during their three-month stay in the beef-lot to gain 400 lbs in weight. The waste produced is 50 lbs of urine and manure a day, which is left untreated in lagoons.[14]

CONCERNS FOR CATTLE

Although the general public rarely get concerned about the welfare of cattle in intensive farming systems (except when human life is threatened), for many people the intensive production of veal causes revulsion. The aim of intensive veal producers around the world is to put young calves (usually dairy-bred males, as they are surplus to requirement) into crates so that they cannot expend any energy or develop any muscles, in order to keep their flesh tender. Calves are denied fresh water, and instead are fed a milk substitute in large quantities. They are also denied access to fibrous food so that their flesh remains white (forage is rich in iron, which darkens the flesh). The calves are kept for up to sixteen weeks in this confinement, sometimes in darkness.

Veal production was first developed in Holland, but soon spread throughout Europe. High-profile writers, such as Mrs Beeton in her *Book of Household Management* (1861), highlighted the practices employed in England to retain the whiteness of

the calves' flesh. She described as 'inhuman and disgraceful' the daily bleeding of the 'Staggering Bobs' to ensure that they remained anaemic to 'please the epicurean taste of vitiated appetites'.[15]

The same abhorrence is seen later in the first exposé of British 'factory farming' in Ruth Harrison's *Animal Machines* (1964), although calves were no longer bled. She documented the plight of the defenceless, brown-eyed 'bobby' calf confined to a small dark crate. And Peter Singer, the Australian philosopher, nominated the quality veal industry as the 'most morally repugnant' of all 'factory farming':

> . . . it represents an extreme, both in the degree of exploitation to which it subjects the animals and in its

Veal crates, like these photographed in 1995 in France (the calves were shipped from Britain), are now banned throughout the European Union and also in the state of Arizona.

absurd inefficiency as a method of providing people with nourishment.[16]

In England, animal rights campaigns encouraged emotions to run particularly high during 1995 when, although veal crates had been banned in the UK in 1990, 426,000 British calves a year were being shipped to Holland and France. A middle-aged librarian from Brighton recorded her reaction to seeing calves arriving in trucks at Seaford ferry terminal in Sussex: 'It makes me think with a shudder of the Nazi cattle trucks',[17] and in January 1995 a woman was crushed to death by a lorry delivering calves to Baginton Airport, near Coventry, destined for the Netherlands.

It's understandable that calves provoke such emotion in our civilized and cultured society; their dark, liquid eyes resemble those of sad, human children, and child protesters at the ferry ports held homemade banners of calves with the slogan 'I want my Mummy'.[18]

TRANSPORT: THE SECRET, DARK SIDE

It is not just calves that have provoked calls for compassion, but cattle being transported and slaughtered in general. At such times cattle are most at the mercy of humans, and generally these people are not those who have reared, or cared for, the cattle.

The worst abuses, nowadays, are frequently captured on camera by undercover animal rights campaigners and broadcast to the world via the internet. For example, 'Animals Australia' campaigns against the live export of Australian cattle via ship to Egypt, where they are slaughtered inhumanely, despite reassurances to the contrary.[19] Although the images of these practices are truly horrific, the workers involved seem to find nothing wrong with the way they treat the cattle, apparently regarding them as mere objects.

But probably the most disturbing for Western, Hindu, Jainist and Buddist eyes is the 'death march' of Indian cattle to slaughterhouses, where they are killed for their hides. The campaign by 'People for the Ethical Treatment of Animals' (PETA) highlights the treatment of India's sacred cow in a film called *Skins Trade*, narrated by Pamela Anderson Lee.[20]

Indian leather is worth $1.7 billion in exports, and the largest markets are Germany, the UK and the US. Although India has welfare legislation in place, the 'bribery and corruption' involved in the trade leads to officials turning a blind eye to some really distressing scenes. Many cattle die en route from their horrific injuries.

While audiences in the 'civilized' world watch with disgust at man's actions, it is worth noting that the 'animal-loving' UK was once well known for its cruelty to cattle, although nowadays the UK has the highest welfare standards in the world. The first ever animal protection movement in England was The Liverpool Society for Preventing Wanton Cruelty to Brute Animals, which targeted the drovers' brutality towards cattle in 1809.

Similar scenes were seen at Smithfield Market in London, which had been on the same site since medieval times. The market was criss-crossed by roads and public thoroughfares and by the early 1800s it was chaotic and overcrowded. Farmers, graziers, salesmen, butchers and members of the public signed a petition and presented it to the Privy Council in 1808 to move the market to a new site, giving the following reasons:

cattle often bruise and lame, and sometimes trample upon and kill each other, by being confined for hours together in a crowded state in the market; and some of

Indian cattle are sold to butchers on the Tamil Nadu / Kerala border because Kerala, having a sizeable Christian population, is one of the only states in India where beef can be bought.

them are maimed and or bruised in a shocking manner by the wagons, carts, or drays driven though Smithfield during market hours; – That the buyers cannot go between or among the beasts in their very crowded state at market to examine them, without danger of sustaining serious bodily injury.[21]

In these noisy, congested conditions it was almost inevitable that the exhausted, bewildered and frightened cattle would be beaten cruelly to get them to the market and then on to meet their fate in the slaughterhouses which surrounded the Smithfield site. Even at night the local residents were kept awake 'as the dreadful blows inflicted on the cattle are distinctly heard in their bedrooms'.[22] It was said that those who sold their cattle for market would not recognize their animals after four days of them being in the city.

Eventually a Royal Commission was established in 1849 to decide the fate of Smithfield, and in 1855 Smithfield closed and the Metropolitan Cattle Market opened at Islington to take advantage of the new rail links, allowing disembarked cattle to be driven the short distance to their sale without having to traverse the London streets.

The highly visible cruelty of the drovers was in direct contrast to the behind-closed-doors treatment of cattle during sea transportation and at the slaughterhouses. It was up to the RSPCA, and especially the Humanitarian League in the 1890s, to expose 'the iniquities which are daily and nightly perpetrated in the sacred name of Trade'.[23] The League described, in pamphlet form, the horrors of the privately owned slaughterhouses,[24] and the transportation of cattle by sea from Ireland, America and Canada.

'A Night View of Smithfield Market, London', from an issue of *The Animals' Friend*, 1838. Note the fallen, exhausted animals on the left being beaten to make them move.

The eyewitness accounts in both publications are, as the authors of *Cattle Ships and our Meat Supply* (1894) state, enough to induce vegetarianism. One particular section asks readers to place themselves on the ships during a stormy nights crossing from Ireland:

> . . . a lurching vessel constantly skipping seas, hold and 'tween decks packed full of terrified and exhausted animals, their foothold slippery and insecure, the air foul, and in total, or almost total, darkness.[25]

But, the authors point out, before the cattle reach this stage they have been cruelly driven to the ports, been without hay or water for hours (or days) and branded. To get onto the ships and into the hold, they have been beaten and driven up and down steep, slippery gangways. The few men in charge of the cattle were often drunk or seasick, and 'usually of a very rough and careless class; the work is irregular and tends to brutalise'.[26]

It was actually butchers who originally pushed to improve conditions on the Irish cattle boats, because of the poor quality of the cattle carcasses and hides due to bruising. But evidence of broken ribs and legs, cows calving in transit and blindness due to the ammoniac fumes in the hold, were enough to bring in regulations.

SLAUGHTER

Since 1861 live cattle arriving in England had been slaughtered at the notorious Deptford slaughterhouses,[27] and in the United States the slaughtering conditions in Chicago were just as inhumane.

An idea of the scale of the scene at Chicago's stockyards can be gained from Upton Sinclair's novel *The Jungle* (1906), which

Knocking (stunning) cattle before slaughter, c. 1906 at Swift and Co.'s Packing House, Chicago.

exposed the practices of Chicago's meatpacking industry. Sinclair himself visited Chicago and worked there for about seven weeks in the winter of 1904. He was confronted by the following vision of the stockyards (as described in his novel):

There is over a square mile of space in the yards, and more than half of it is occupied by cattle pens; north and south as far as the eye can reach there stretches a sea of pens. And they were all filled – so many cattle no one had ever dreamed existed in the world. Red cattle, black, white, and yellow cattle; old cattle and young cattle; great bellowing bulls and little calves not an hour born; meek-

Bleeding the cow after death; the Villette slaughterhouse, Paris, 1907.

'Dropping hides' and 'splitting chucks' in the Beef Department of Swift and Co.'s Packing House, c. 1906.

eyed milch cows and fierce, long-horned Texas steers. The sound of them here was as of all the barnyards of the universe; and as for counting them – it would have taken all day simply to count the pens.[28]

From their pens, the cattle were driven up fifteen-feet wide walkways into chutes raised high above the pens. These chutes carried a continuous stream of unsuspecting cattle to their deaths – 'a very river of death'.[29] Sinclair did not spare the sensibilities of his reader with his description of the actual killing of the cattle (neither does Sterchi's *The Cow*), and he admired the skills of the workers and the pace at which the cattle were dispatched:

Along one side of the room ran a narrow gallery, a few feet from the floor, into which gallery the cattle were driven by men with goads which gave them electric shocks. Once crowded in here, the creatures were prisoned, each in a separate pen, by gates that shut, leaving them no room to turn around; and while they stood bellowing and plunging, over the top of the pen there leaned one of the 'knockers', armed with a sledge hammer, and watching for a chance to deal a blow. The room echoed with the thuds in quick succession, and the stamping and kicking of the steers.[30]

After each cow had been knocked unconscious, another man would raise a lever and the side of each pen would rise, allowing the animal, still struggling and kicking, to slide out on to the 'killing bed'. Here, another man attached shackles to one of the cow's hind legs and hoisted it upside down above the killing bed. The 'butcher' then slit the cow's throat and they were left to bleed for several minutes; just enough time for the 'knocker' to stun the next fifteen to twenty animals.

Abattoirs in modern America are different places since animal welfare legislation has been introduced, but there are still welfare concerns. Eric Schlosser describes an unnamed slaughterhouse on the High Plains which processes 5,000 head a day. There appears to be less stress on the cattle as they arrive at the slaughterhouse entrance, having walked along specially designed corrals that funnel them down into a single line.[31] They stroll down a narrow chute into the slaughterhouse, oblivious to what is about to happen. Once in the building, they are blocked by a gate where, instead of using a sledgehammer, the 'knocker' stands over them and shoots a captive bolt stunner at the animal's forehead.

While the old meatpacking plants in Chicago could slaughter about 50 cattle an hour, modern plants despatch 400 cattle an hour (six animals every minute). It is difficult to guarantee that every cow is properly stunned when processing such a huge number.

GUILT AND MORALITY

Maybe because of our once-close relationship with cattle, there has always been a certain guilt felt when killing useful cattle (see the *bouphonia* in chapter Four). The way cattle are treated as objects has been used by commentators and humanitarians as a metaphor for the way society treats sections of society.

Although the term 'cattle' has been historically used to describe all livestock, the political theorist James Harrington (1611–1677) thought the Scottish people were oppressed because they were 'little better than the cattle of the nobility'; and in Victorian times it was thought to be a 'barbarous practice' that 'men and women should stand in droves, like cattle, for inspection' at hiring-fairs.[32] Currently, we use the term 'cattle market' to describe a place, usually a nightclub, where men go to ogle sexually attractive females or to find a sexual partner.

Equating the abused cow with an abused person can be seen in both Sinclair's *The Jungle* and Sterchi's *The Cow*. These novels carry a moral message about social injustice and the dehumanizing effect of capitalist production. But Sterchi uses the fate of a particular cow, Blösch, as a direct parallel to that of an immigrant abattoir worker, Ambrosio, who after seven years of hard labour finds himself killing the animal he had once admired. Human and cow (ruined by overwork and modern dairy production, respectively) are one and the same:

> But *caramba!* The emaciated body that had been dragged out of the cattle-truck onto the ramp, that had mooed so pathetically into the morning mist, that body was also Ambrosio's body. Blösch's wounds were his own wounds, the lost lustre of her hide was his loss, the deep furrows between her ribs, the hat-sized hollows round her hips, they were dug into his flesh, what had been taken from the cow had been taken from himself. Blösch's limping and dragging and hesitating, that was him. Ambrosio himself on a halter. Yes, he had laughed at Knuchel's cows for their passivity and meekness, but the display of unconditional obedience, of obsequiousness and motiveless mooing that he had witnessed on the ramp, he had also witnessed them in himself, to his own disgust. In Blösch on that Tuesday morning, Ambrosio had recognized himself.[33]

Similarly, a Czech *samizdat* (anti-government) cartoon from the 1990s shows two women staring sadly at a factory farm packed full of cows. One is saying 'I remember the days when cows had souls', to which her companion replies, 'Yes, and so did we'.[34]

The metaphor of men and slaves as cattle has been around for a long time. Black slaves were often described as 'black cattle', and the war poet Wilfred Owen (1893–1918) describes in his 'Anthem for Doomed Youth' (1917) the young soldiers as cattle going to slaughter in the face of the enemy's guns:

> What passing-bells for these who die as cattle?
> Only the monstrous anger of the guns.[35]

The innocence of the soldiers, herded together and blindly following each other towards the certainty of death; men being so easily disposed of, without thought for their humanity or individuality.

Epilogue: Out of Sight, Out of Mind?

Having charted the deterioration of the human/cow relationship in the West, is there any way in which it can be rebuilt? We seem to have reduced the epitome of virility, fertility and strength to a mere sperm donor, the Mother and nourisher of the world to a mere milk machine and the strong, willing ox into a beef-and-leather factory. Cattle are regarded as objects and have been shunted to the periphery of our lives; only a few people are privileged to interact positively with cattle and witness their behaviour.

It is unlikely that cattle will meet the same fate as their aurochs ancestors, as people will always want to eat beef, drink milk and wear leather; cattle have become firmly entrenched in our world. But do we need to use the cow in such a mercenary fashion?

The first hurdle to rebuilding the relationship is getting people to even think about the cow, let alone about how their eating and shopping habits impact on the cow's life. While cartoonists such as Gary Larson keep us laughing at cows (because, yes, they are innately funny), it is also important to introduce children and teenagers to the real live cow as part of their education – after all, they are the shoppers and consumers of the future.

It is essential for us to recognize what we are asking cattle to do for us; once this effort is acknowledged, then they will surely regain our respect. Open farm days, urban farms and school

Phoenix the calf, survivor of a foot and mouth disease precautionary slaughter in Devon, England, 2001: the closest thing we have to a modern mystical cow?

farms should be encouraged, and visited; which will, hopefully, prevent many of the misconceptions surrounding cows, such as where milk comes from – no, it is not the supermarket![1]

Children need to learn more than just the fact that cows go *moo*. One novel way of reconnecting the naïve urbanite with the cow is by harnessing the power of the media. For example, an American website (sadly, no longer active) called 'Cow Cam' provided a Longhorn's-eye view of life, via a wireless camera which was attached to the animal's neck collar. The site proudly announced: 'A first in bovine history . . . the Cow Cam' and offered 'Streaming Cow Cams from the cow's point of view' urging visitors to 'Read blogs, watch cows: be a part of everyday cow life'.[2]

And while there are still people interested in preserving and publicizing the cultural history of the cow, bull and ox, then there is a chance that these animals will remain as part of our heritage. Non-profitable organizations such as the American Livestock Breeds Conservancy and the UK's Rare Breeds Survival Trust are working hard to preserve endangered cattle breeds, particularly those which have historical or cultural associations with particular countries or regions.

So could there be a happier future for cattle? Will they all be reared on grain and beer, and be routinely massaged with sake, like the Japanese Wagyu cattle, who produce the gourmet Kobe beef, are reported to be? Definitely not, but we have a responsibility to look again at our treatment of cattle: we brought them into being, killing off their wild ancestors in the process, and they have played such a huge role in shaping early civilizations and our modern world – we just need reminding sometimes.

Timeline of the Cow

c. 2 million BC

Bos primigenius or aurochs, the progenitor of domestic cattle, evolve in Asia

c. 250,000 BC

Aurochs reach Europe, having previously migrated into the Middle East and north-east Africa

c. 6,000 to c. 4,000 BC

Humans domesticate aurochs in three separate areas of the Old World

c. 3,200 BC

In Mesopotamia, a stylized symbol to denote the word 'ox' is developed, and the plough and ox-cart are invented

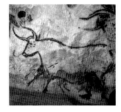

1627

The last aurochs dies in Poland; the species becomes the first documented case of animal extinction

1647

Paulus Potter creates the epitome of cattle paintings, *The Bull*

1726

Francisco Romero becomes the father of modern bullfighting, introducing fighting on foot rather than on horseback

1780s

Robert Bakewell 'creates' the Improved Longhorn cattle breed which kickstarts the British cattle industry

1932

Ernest Hemingway's *Death in The Afternoon* is published – an introduction for many to the *corrida*

1960s

The *Concrete Cows* appear in Milton Keynes

1994

The Rwandan Genocide is the culmination of decades of conflict between Hutu and Tutsi groups, the history of which is rooted in issues over cattle ownership

c. 2,500 BC	*c.* 1,500 BC	*c.* 50 BC	1086	1493
Domestic cattle export trade begins between the Near East, India and Africa	Aryans bring their creator bull-gods and cows to India, greatly influencing Hindu literature	Julius Caesar encounters the aurochs in Germany and domestic cattle are described by Varro Reatinus as the 'origin of all money'	The unit of measurement used in the *Domesday Book* is based on the work rate of a team of ploughing oxen	Christopher Columbus ships Spanish cattle to Hispaniola in the West Indies

1788	1835	1867	1920S
First cattle arrive in Australia at Port Jackson, alongside the first shipment of English convicts to the British colony	Bull-baiting is made illegal in England	The first Texan Longhorns are driven up the Chisholm Trail, marking the beginning of the US beef cattle boom	Heinz and Lutz Heck attempt to recreate the aurochs from 'primitive forms' of domestic cattle

1994	1996	1999	2006
Bovine growth hormones are used commercially in the US to boost dairy cow milk yields	BSE halts British beef exports	Beat Sterchi's novel *The Cow* is published	Veal crates are banned throughout the EU and Arizona in the USA

References

INTRODUCTION: REINTRODUCING THE COW, BULL AND OX

1 According to The Food and Agriculture Organization of the
   United Nations (FAO) statistics for 2005,
   http://faostat.fao.org/site/396/default.aspx (live animal production figures) (accessed 1 October 2006).
2 A. Wünschmann 'The Wild and Domestic Oxen', in *Grzimek's
   Animal Life Encyclopaedia*, vol. XIII: *Mammals IV* (New York, 1972),
   p. 368.
3 The full list can be seen at www.arrakis.es/~eledu/justcows.htm.
4 See 'Cattle and the Global Environmental Crisis' chapter in
   Jeremy Rifkin, *Beyond Beef: The Rise and Fall of the Cattle Culture*
   (London, 1992), pp. 185–230.

1 WILD OX TO DOMESTICATES

1 See the Paleontologisk Museum, University of Oslo, website at
   www.toyen.uio.no/palmus/galleri/montre/english/a31922.htm
   (accessed 30 August 2006).
2 Daniel G. Bradley, 'Genetic Hoof Prints: The DNA Trail Leading
   Back to the Origins of Today's Cattle Has Taken Some Surprising
   Turns Along the Way', *Natural History* (February 2003).
3 See R. Schloeth's studies of wild Camargue cattle for further
   insights into the probable behaviours and personality of the aurochs
   in Wünschmann, 'The Wild and Domestic Oxen', pp. 332–4. Also
   see Thomas Bewick, *A General History of Quadrupeds* (Newcastle
   upon Tyne, 1790), pp. 38–41.

4 André Leroi-Gourhan, 'Animals of the Old Stone Age', in A. Houghton Brodrick, ed., *Animals in Archaeology* (London, 1972), p. 8.

5 Wünschmann. 'The Wild and Domestic Oxen', p. 370.

6 Quoted in Cis van Vuure, *Retracing the Aurochs* (Sofia and Moscow, 2005), p. 240.

7 Caroline Grigson (1981), cited in Simon J. M. Davis, *The Archaeology of Animals* (London, 1987), p. 175.

8 See views of Linda Donley-Reid and Ian Hodder on aurochs symbolism at Catal Huyuk, Turkey, in Michael Balter, *The Goddess and the Bull* (London, 2005), pp. 323–4.

9 Inscription no. 34 from an octagonal prism and clay fragments discovered at Kalah-Shergat, currently in the British Museum, trans. H. Rawlinson, at www.bible-history.com/assyria_archaeology/archaeology_of_ancient_assyria_text_tiglath_pileser_i.html (accessed 22 May 2006).

10 H. Epstein and Ian L. Mason, 'Cattle', in Mason, ed., *Evolution of Domesticated Animals* (London, 1984), p. 8.

11 For the full record of the event, see www.nefertiti.iwebland.com/timelines/topics/fishing_and_hunting.htm (accessed 11 May 2006).

12 Hunting contributed to the extinction of the aurochs in Egypt, but other causes included the increasing aridity of the fertile savannah and the drying up of rivers and streams. Aurochs also had to compete for grazing with their domesticated descendents.

13 Julius Caesar, *The Gallic War*, trans. Carolyn Hammond (Oxford, 1996), 6:28, pp. 132–3.

14 See the letter written by the Polish scientist Anton Schmeenerger to the Polish naturalist Gesner in van Vuure, *Retracing the Aurochs*, p. 385.

15 Van Vuure, *Retracing the Aurochs*, p. 72.

16 Juliet Clutton-Brock, *A Natural History of Domesticated Mammals* (London, 1999), p. 84.

17 F. E. Zeuner, 'The History of the Domestication of Cattle', in A. E. Mourant and F. E. Zeuner, eds, *Man and Cattle: Proceedings of a Symposium on Domestication*, Royal Anthropological Institute Occasional Paper no. 18 (1963), p. 10.

18 Charles Darwin, *Voyage of the Beagle* (reprinted New York, 2002), p. 200.

19 Gilbert White, *The Natural History and Antiquities of Selborne* (reprinted London, 1993), p. 194.

20 See text in Miriam Lichtheim, *Ancient Egyptian Literature*, vol. III (Berkeley, CA, 1980), p. 158.

21 Varro Reatinus, *Varro on Farming*, trans. Lloyd Storr-Best (London, 1912), Book 2:1.11.

22 Hammurabi's Code of Laws, trans. L. W. King, http://eawc.evans ville.edu/anthology/hammurabi.htm (accessed 22 May 2006). For a discussion of cattle in the Visigothic laws, see also Joyce Salisbury, *The Beast Within: Animals in the Middle Ages* (London, 1994), p. 19.

23 Bradley, 'Genetic hoof prints'.

24 Pliny the Elder, *The Natural History of Pliny*, trans. J. Bostock and H. T. Riley (London, 1893), 8:70, p. 2328.

25 Peter Harbison, *Pre-Christian Ireland* (London, 1988), p. 30.

26 Peter Berresford Ellis, *A Brief History of the Celts* (London, 2003), pp. 102, 142.

27 See J. G. Frazer, *The Golden Bough: A Study in Magic and Religion*, abridged edn (reprinted London, 1987), chap. 62: 'The Fire-Festivals of Europe', pp. 609–41.

28 Gervase Markham in Joanna Swabe, *Animals, Disease and Human Society* (London, 1999), p. 82.

29 Jared Diamond, *Guns, Germs and Steel* (London, 1998), pp. 206–7.

30 Ibid., p. 213.

31 Virginia de John Anderson, *Creatures of Empire: How Domesticated Animals Transformed Early America* (Oxford, 2004), p. 77.

32 Ibid., pp. 107–8.

33 Herodotus, *The Histories*, trans. Aubrey de Sélincourt (London, 1996), 3:111, p. 197.

34 Ibid., 4:69, p. 237.

2 BULL-GODS, BULL-KINGS

1 *The Epic of Gilgamesh*, trans. Andrew George (London, 2000), p. 2.

2 W. M. O'Neil, *Early Astronomy from Babylonia to Copernicus* (Sydney, 1986), p. 154.

3 See Cyril Aldred, *The Egyptians* (London, 1998), p. 77.

4 Herodotus, *The Histories*, 3:28, p. 165.

5 See Jack Randolph Conrad, *The Horn and the Sword: The History of the Bull as a Symbol of Power and Fertility* (London, 1959), p. 54.

6 Ralph T. H. Griffith, trans., *The Hymns of the Rig-veda* (Senares, 1889) 1:33.10–11.

7 Ibid.,10:103.1.

8 *The Golden Bough*, p. 351.

9 The fictional character of Valerius is a devotee of Mithras in Manda Scott's *Boudica: Dreaming The Bull* (London, 2004). See especially pp. 224–37, where Valerius tries to prevent his god, in bull form, from being baited.

10 Pliny the Elder, *Natural History: A Selection*, trans. John F. Healy (London, 1991), p. 216.

11 Berresford Ellis, *A Brief History of the Celts*, p. 30.

12 Pennethorne Hughes, *Witchcraft* (London, 1952), p. 91.

13 Cited in Charles Squire, *Celtic Myth and Legend* (New York, 2003), p. 175.

14 Virgil, *The Georgics*, trans. Robert Wells (Manchester, 1982), Georgic 3, pp. 68–9.

15 The Cretan Bull and Minotaur myths are as described in Robert Graves, *The Greek Myths* (London, 1992): no. 88 Minos and his Brothers; no. 98 Theseus in Crete; and no. 129 The Seventh Labour: The Cretan Bull.

16 See J. D. Evans, 'Cretan Cattle-Cults and Sports', in Mourant and Zeuner, eds, *Man and Cattle*, pp. 140–41; and Mary Renault, *The King Must Die* (London, 1958), for a fictional account of 'The Bull Dance' held at 'The Bull Court' in Knossos.

17 The life of Lane Frost, the world-champion bull rider in 1987, is portrayed in the film *8 Seconds* (1994).

18 More details about bull-riding can be found on the Professional Bull Riders website at www.pbrnow.com.

19 'A Day in the Life of J. W. Hart, interviewed by Bridget Freer in

the *Sunday Times Magazine* (12 March 2006).

20 More information about the bull-running can be found at www.spanish-fiestas.com/spanish-festivals/pamplona-bull-running-san-fermin.htm (accessed 7 October 2006).

21 Ernest Hemingway, *The Sun Always Rises* (New York, 1926), pp. 203–4.

22 See www.jallikatu.com/index1.htm (accessed 22 August 2006).

23 See bull-racing in Michael Palin, *Himalaya* (London, 2004), p. 23.

24 See article on www.taipeitimes.com/News/feat/archives/2005/03/29/2003248 280 (accessed 22 August 2006).

25 Alan Baker, *The Gladiator: The Secret History of Rome's Warrior Slaves* (London, 2000), p. 100.

26 See Keith Thomas, *Man and the Natural World: Changing Attitudes in England, 1500–1800* (London, 1983), p. 93.

27 Maureen Waller, *1700: Scenes from London Life* (London, 2000), p. 223.

28 Cited in E. J. Burford, *London: The Synfulle Citie* (London, 1990), p. 181.

29 Ibid.

30 Cited in Harriet Ritvo, *The Animal Estate: The English and Other Creatures in the Victorian Age* (Cambridge, MA, 1987), pp. 125–6.

31 See Keith Tester, *Animals and Society* (London, 1992), pp. 101–9.

32 Pliny the Elder, *The Natural History of Pliny*, 8:70, p. 2329.

33 See Allen Josephs, 'Hemingway's Spanish Sensibility', in Scott Donaldson, ed., *Ernest Hemingway* (Cambridge, 1996), p. 229.

34 John Richardson, *A Life of Picasso*, vol. II (London, 1996), p. 242.

35 Adrian Shubert, *Death and Money in the Afternoon* (Oxford, 1999), p. 8.

36 For an analysis of *Tauromaquia*, see Robert Hughes, *Goya* (New York, 2003), pp. 351–65.

37 See Garry Marvin, *Bullfight* (Oxford, 1988), pp. 87–8.

38 Ibid., p. 99.

39 Ernest Hemingway, *Death in the Afternoon* (London, 1932), p. 94.

40 See Pierre Daix, *Picasso: Life and Art*, trans. Olivia Emmet (London,

1993), pp. 230–31.

41 Jonathan Burt, *Animals in Film* (London, 2002), pp. 119 and 133.

3 COW MYSTICISM AND A RURAL IDYLL

1 Thomas, *Man and the Natural World*, p. 118.

2 Ibid., p. 98.

3 Beat Sterchi, *The Cow* (London, 1999), p. 87.

4 Ogden Nash, *I Wouldn't Have Missed It* (London, 1983), p. 19.

5 See E. O. James, *The Ancient Gods* (London, 1999), pp. 85–6.

6 For a modern re-working of cow folklore, see Marlene Newman, *Myron's Magic Cow* (Bath, 2005).

7 More details about Daisy the cow can be found at www.chicago history.org/fire/oleary.

8 Jack Malvern, 'Cow-tipping Myth Hasn't Got a Leg To Stand On', *The Times* (5 November 2005), p. 5.

9 More information can be found at www.swissinfo.org/eng/ travel/detail/Locking_horns_in_canton_Valais.html?siteSect=411 &sid=1760102&cKey=1050223500000 (accessed 22 August 2006).

10 'Mother Instinct Makes Sucklers a Real Threat', *Farmers Weekly*, 'Farm Health and Safety Supplement' (11 October 2002), p. s8.

11 Griffith trans., *Hymns of the Rig-veda*, 1:153.3.

12 Deryck O. Lodrick, *Sacred Cows, Sacred Places* (London, 1981), pp. 52–3.

13 Ibid., p. 67.

14 Indira Gandhi quoted in Oriana Fallaci, 'Indira's Coup', *New York Review of Books*, 18 September 1975.

15 Also see 'Mother Cow' chapter in Marvin Harris, *Cows, Pigs, Wars and Witches* (New York, 1989) for his views on modern 'cow worship' in India.

16 Norman Lewis, *A Goddess in the Stones: Travels in India* (London, 1991), p. 38.

17 Sterchi, *The Cow*, p. 95.

18 White, *The Natural History and Antiquities of Selborne*, p. 23.

19 Charles Dickens, *Dombey and Son* (reprinted London, 2002), p. 320.

20 D. H. Lawrence, *Reflections on the Death of a Porcupine* (Philadelphia, PA, 1925), pp. 203, 164 and 166 (respectively).

21 Ibid., p. 167.

22 Ibid., p. 166.

23 Ibid., p. 176.

24 Ibid., p. 167.

25 Ibid., p. 165.

26 Norman MacCaig, *Collected Poems* (London, 1993), p. 117.

27 Cited in William Vaughan, *British Painting: The Golden Age* (London, 1999), p. 154.

28 Cited in Hilda Kean, *Animal Rights* (London, 1998), p. 49.

29 For a description of the dairymaids' symbolic role in urban May Day rituals, see Charles Phythian-Adams, 'Milk and Soot: The Changing Vocabulary of a Popular Ritual in Stuart and Hanoverian London', in Derek Fraser and Anthony Sutcliffe, eds, *The Pursuit of Urban History* (London, 1983).

30 Thomas Hardy, *Tess of the D'Urbervilles* (reprinted London, 1985), p. 176.

31 Ibid., p. 208.

32 See 'Cattle' chapter in Philip Hook and Mark Poltimore, *Popular Nineteenth Century Paintings: A Dictionary of European Genre Painters* (London, 1986).

33 See Mariët Nestermann, *The Art of the Dutch Republic, 1585–1718* (London, 1996), pp. 107–8.

34 See Colin Rhodes, *Primitivism and Modern Art* (London, 1997), pp. 144–5.

35 Mark Rosenthal, *Franz Marc* (Munich, 1989), pp. 20–21.

36 John Betjeman, *Collected Poems* (reprinted London, 2000), p. 20.

37 The official website of CowParade can be found at www.cowparade.com.

38 See Edward McPherson, *Buster Keaton: Tempest in a Flat Hat* (London, 2004), pp. 168–71.

39 Nell Dunn, *Poor Cow* (reprinted London, 1988), p. 141.

4 TOILING THE FIELDS AND A 'CATTLE COMPLEX'

1　See Andrew Sherratt, 'Plough and Pastoralism: Aspects of the
　　Secondary Products Revolution', in Ian Hodder, Glynn Isaac and
　　Norman Hammond, eds, *Pattern of the Past: Studies in Honour of
　　David Clarke* (Cambridge, 1981), pp. 261–301.
2　Cited in Garry Marvin, *Bullfight* (Oxford, 1988), p. 91.
3　Hesiod, *The Works and Days*, trans. Richmond Lattimore
　　(Ann Arbor, MI, 1959), 437–40, p. 71.
4　Ibid., 814–16, p. 155.
5　Virgil, *The Georgics*, trans. Robert Wells, *Georgic* 3, pp. 66–7.
6　Varro Reatinus, *Varro on Farming*, Book 1:20.1.
7　Columella, *On Agriculture*, vol. III, trans E. S. Forster and Edward
　　H. Heffner (Cambridge, 1954), 6:1:1–2. p. 125.
8　Paul Starkey, 'The History of Working Animals in Africa', in
　　R. M. Blench and K. MacDonald, eds, *The Origins and
　　Development of African Livestock* (London, 2000), pp. 478–502; or
　　www.animaltraction.com/StarkeyPapers/Starkey-History
　　AnimalTractioninAfrica-97-draft.pdf (accessed 9 June 2006).
9　John Lockwood Kipling, *Beast and Man in India*, cited in J. Frank
　　Dobie, *The Longhorns* (London, 1943), p. xiii.
10　Cited in Anderson, *Creatures of Empire: How Domesticated Animals
　　Transformed Early America* , p. 145.
11　R. Welldon Finn, *Domesday Book: A Guide* (Chichester, 1973), p. 66.
12　W.H.R. Curtler *A Short History of English Agriculture* (Oxford,
　　1909), p. 16.
13　See 'Ox' entry at www.bestiary.ca/beasts/beastalphashort.htm
　　(accessed 24 May 2006).
14　Aesop, *The Complete Fables* (reprinted London, 1998), p. 73.
15　Frazer, *The Golden Bough*, p. 466.
16　Francis Galton, *The Art of Travel* (reprinted London, 1971), p. 58.
17　Ibid., p. 60.
18　Ibid., p. 64.
19　Ibid., pp. 252–3.
20　Cited in Christopher Hibbert, *Africa Explored: Europeans in the*

Dark Continent, 1769–1889 (London, 1982), p. 237.

21 See E. E. Evans-Pritchard, *The Nuer* (Oxford, 1974), p. 49.

22 See discussion in the Introduction of Jonathan Mtetwa, *Man and Cattle in Africa* (Saarbrücken, 1982).

23 Philip M. Peek and Kwesi Yankah, eds, *African Folklore: An Encyclopedia* (London, 2004), p. 4.

24 Ibid., p. 79.

25 Derrick J. Stenning, 'Africa: The Social Background', in Mourant and Zeuner, eds, *Man and Cattle*, p. 112.

26 Michael E. Meeker, *The Pastoral Son and the Spirit of Patriarch: Religion, Society, and Person among East African Stockkeepers* (Madison, WI, 1989), p. 18.

27 Cited in Melville J. Herskovits, *The Cattle Complex in East Africa* (n.p., 1927), p. 72.

28 Frazer, *The Golden Bough*, p. 565.

29 Taken from Patrick Cunningham, 'Maasai Rite of Passage', *Geographical*, LXXVIII/3 (March 2006), pp. 26–32.

30 See Mtetwa, *Man and Cattle in Africa*, pp. 230–1.

31 See Martin Meredith, *The State of Africa: A History of Fifty Years of Independence* (London, 2005), p. 158.

32 J. Terrence McCabe, *Cattle Bring Us to Our Enemies* (Ann Arbor, MI, 2004), p. 93.

33 Ibid., p. 94.

34 John Iliffe, *Africans: The History of a Continent* (Cambridge, 1995), p. 210.

35 See Mtetwa, *Man and Cattle in Africa*, pp. 11–12.

36 Diamond, *Guns, Germs and Steel*, p. 186.

37 Figures from M. Mackenzie, *The Empire of Nature: Hunting, Conservation and British Imperialism* (Manchester, 1988), p. 241.

38 Figures cited in 'Inner Mongolia near Starvation', *BBC Online*, 25 January 2001, http://news.bbc.co.uk/1/hi/world/asia-pacific/1135850.stm.

5 CATTLE STARS AND ROMANTIC ASSOCIATIONS

1 Henri Misson, *Memoirs and Observations of Travels over England* (London, 1719), pp. 310–11.

2 Cited in Richard Perren, *The Meat Trade in Britain, 1840–1914* (London, 1978), p. 32.

3 Cited in Raymond B. Becker, *Dairy Cattle Breeds* (Gainesville, FL, 1973), p. 64.

4 Cited in Stephen Hall and Juliet Clutton-Brock, *Two Hundred Years of British Farm Livestock* (London, 1989), p. 63.

5 Becker, *Dairy Cattle Breeds*, p. 64.

6 Reverend Arthur Young, *General View of the Agriculture of the County of Sussex* (London, 1813), p. 228.

7 Ben Rogers, *Beef and Liberty: Roast Beef, John Bull and the English Nation* (London, 2004), p. 15.

8 For a complete history of the Shorthorn breed, see www.shorthorn.co.uk/beef_shorthorn/history.htm.

9 Cited in Harriet Ritvo, *The Animal Estate: The English and Other Creatures in the Victorian Age*, p. 56.

10 Ibid., see 'The Critique of Fat Cattle', pp. 69–79.

11 Cited in William Vaughan, *British Painting: The Golden Age* (London, 1999), p. 165.

12 James Dickson, 'On the Application of the Points by which Livestock are Judged', *Quarterly Review of Agriculture*, VI (1835/6), p. 269.

13 Cited in Perren, *The Meat Trade in Britain*, p. 32.

14 See J. Frank Dobie, *The Longhorns* (London, 1943), p. 292.

15 Cited in Clyde A. Milner II, Carol A. O'Connor and Martha A. Sandweiss, eds, *The Oxford History of the American West* (Oxford, 1994), p. 252.

16 For a full description of the Chicago stockyards, see 'Annihilating Space', meat chapter in William Cronon, *Nature's Metropolis: Chicago and the Great West* (London, 1991), pp. 207–59.

17 J. Frank Dobie, *Cow People* (Austin, TX, 1981), p. 32.

18 Cited in Lonn Taylor and Ingrid Maar, *The American Cowboy*

(Washington, DC, 1983), p. 27.

19 Andy Adams, cited in Jon E. Lewis, *The Mammoth Book of The West* (London, 2001), p. 163.

20 Ibid., p. 164.

21 George C. Duffield, 'Driving Cattle from Texas to Iowa, 1866', in *Annals of Iowa 14* (1924), pp. 252–4.

22 The mass slaughter of millions of buffalo, mainly for their hides, which Philadelphian tanners could turn into commercial leather, removed the livelihood of the Native Americans, gradually forcing them into Government reserves. The expansion of the open range cattle industry was the final nail in the coffin for the Indians. See discussion in Robert V. Hine and John Mack Faragher, *The American West: A New Interpretive History* (New Haven, CT, 2000), p. 317.

23 Cited in Lewis, *The Mammoth Book of The West*, p. 196.

24 Cited in Taylor and Maar, *The American Cowboy*, p. 39.

25 Ibid., p. 36.

26 Ibid., p. 18.

27 See Milner, O'Connor and Sandweiss, eds, *The Oxford History of the American West*, pp. 266–7.

28 A description of the reversal of Longhorn fortunes can be accessed at http://www.tsha.utexas.edu/handbook/online/ articles/LL/atl2.html.

29 D. J. Anthony and W.G.T. Blois, *The Meat Industry*, 2nd edn (London, 1931), pp. 47–75.

30 J. T. Critchell and J. Raymond, *A History of the Frozen Meat Trade* (London, 1912), p. 13.

31 FAOSTAT (classic) statistics for 2005 (Livestock primary production).

32 See Robert Hughes, *The Fatal Shore: A History of the Transportation of Convicts to Australia, 1787–1868* (London, 1987), p. 96.

33 See A.G.L. Shaw, *The Story of Australia*, 5th edn (London, 1983), p. 154.

6 POOR COW: PUSHING THE BOUNDARIES

1 Douglas M. Considine and Glenn D. Considine, eds, *Foods and*

Food Products Encyclopaedia (New York, 1982), p. 1170.

2 FAOSTAT (classic) 2005 figures.

3 Figures from C.J.C. Phillips, *Principles of Cattle Production* (Wallingford, 2001), p. 9, and for 2005/6 from the Milk Development Council website at www.mdcdatum.org.uk/Milk%20Supply/averagemilkyields.html (accessed 21 September 2006).

4 Steve Jones, *Almost Like a Whale* (London, 1999), p. 44.

5 John Webster, *Understanding the Dairy Cow* (Oxford, 1987), p. 22.

6 Figures taken from the University of Reading's Department of Agricultural and Food Economics website at www.apd.rdg.ac.uk/AgEcon/livestockdisease/cattle.htm (accessed 21 September 2006).

7 Eric Schlosser, *Fast Food Nation* (London, 2001), p. 150.

8 Gina Mallet, *Last Chance To Eat: The Fate of Taste in a Fast Food World* (Edinburgh, 2005), p. 118. 'The Ox is Gored' chapter discusses how beef has been tainted by health scares.

9 Cited in Jimmy M. Skaggs, *Prime Cut: Livestock Raising and Meatpacking in the US* (College Station, TX, 1986), pp. 121–2.

10 Brian J. Ford, *BSE: The Facts* (London, 1996), pp. 22–3.

11 Official figures from DEFRA website, www.defra.gov.uk/animalh/bse/general/qa/section1.html#q1 (accessed 22 September 2006), and estimates cited in Michael B. A. Oldstone, *Viruses, Plagues and History* (Oxford, 2000), p. 163.

12 See figures at www.cjd.ed.ac.uk/figures.htm (as accessed 8 March 2007).

13 See FAO document 'Cattle Ranching and Deforestation' at www.fao.org/ag/againfo/resources/documents/pol-briefs/03/EN/AGA04_EN_05.pdf, p. 2.

14 Schlosser, *Fast Food Nation*, p. 150.

15 Isabella Beeton, *Book of Household Management*, abridged edn (reprinted Oxford, 2000), pp. 200–01.

16 Peter Singer, *Animal Liberation*, 2nd edn (London, 1995), p. 129.

17 Alun Howkins and Linda Merricks, 'Dewy-eyed Veal Calves: Live Animal Exports and Middle-Class Opinion, 1980–1995',

Agricultural History Review, xlviii/1 (2000), p. 99.

18 See photograph in *The Independent* (22 April 1995).

19 The Animals Australia campaign can be viewed at www.animals australia.org/default2.asp?idL1=1272&idL2=1865&idL3=1880, and Compassion in World Farming's campaign against long distance transportation can been viewed at www.ciwf.org.uk/ campaigns/primary_campaigns/long_distance.html .

20 *Skins Trade* can be viewed at www.petatv.com/skins.html.

21 Richard Perren, *The Meat Trade in Britain, 1840–1914* (London, 1978), p. 33.

22 Taken from the *Voice of Humanity* (1827), cited in Hilda Kean, *Animal Rights* (London, 1998), p. 62.

23 I. M. Greg and S. H. Towers, *Cattle Ships and our Meat Supply* (London, 1894), p. 3.

24 Horace Francis Lester, *Behind the Scenes in Slaughterhouses* (London, 1892).

25 Greg and Towers, *Cattle Ships and our Meat Supply*, p. 13.

26 Ibid., pp. 11–12.

27 Live cattle were imported and slaughtered at Deptford docks following a disastrous outbreak of rinderpest, which had been bought into Hull by cattle from Russia in 1865.

28 Upton Sinclair, *The Jungle* (reprinted New York, 1986), pp. 40–41.

29 Ibid., p. 42.

30 Ibid., p. 48. In England, the method of slaughter was with a pole-axe which was similar to a sledge-hammer, but on the end of the head was a hollow steel spike. A cane was inserted into the resulting hole made by the blow to stir up the brains of the dying animal; supposedly to improve the taste of the meat.

31 The corrals have been designed by the animal scientist Temple Grandin, whose own experience with autism led her to realize that animals process the world as sensory information – sights and sounds, pictures – just as she does. In her book *Animals in Translation* (London, 2005), she describes her work with cattle to improve the feed-lots and slaughtering handling facilities in the majority of us and Canadian concerns.

32 Examples cited in Thomas, *Man and the Natural World: Changing Attitudes in England, 1500–1800*, p. 48.
33 Sterchi, *The Cow*, p. 354.
34 Cited in Roger Scruton, *Animal Rights and Wrongs*, 3rd edn (London, 2000), p. 103.
35 Wilfred Owen, *The War Poems*, ed. Jon Stallworthy (reprinted London, 2006), p. 12.

EPILOGUE: OUT OF SIGHT, OUT OF MIND?

1 Farmers Weekly website, www.fwi.co.uk, forum pages sometimes relate public misconceptions about milk production: 17 May 2006 saw comments that children thought cows had to be killed to get their milk, and a comment from a mother of three children that their milk comes from the supermarket (not a cow).
2 Another eye-opener was the televised slaughter of beef cattle during the programme *Kill it, Cook it, Eat it* (BBC3, 5 March 2007), which showed the processes involved when taking the live cow to beef on the plate. Many in the audience remarked on the skill of the slaughtermen and how humanely the cattle were treated.

Bibliography

Aldred, Cyril, *The Egyptians* (London, 1998)

Anthony, D. J., and W.G.T. Blois, *The Meat Industry*, 2nd edn (London, 1931)

Balter, Michael, *The Goddess and the Bull* (London, 2005)

Berresford Ellis, Peter, *A Brief History of the Celts* (London, 2003)

Bradley, D. G., 'Genetic Hoof Prints: The DNA Trail Leading Back to the Origins of Today's Cattle Has Taken Some Surprising Turns Along the Way', *Natural History* (February 2003)

Burt, Jonathan, *Animals in Film* (London, 2002)

Clutton-Brock, Juliet, *A Natural History of Domesticated Mammals* (London, 1999)

Conrad, Jack Randolph, *The Horn and the Sword: The History of the Bull as a Symbol of Power and Fertility* (London, 1959)

Cotterell, Arthur, *The Minoan World* (London, 1979)

Critchell, J. T., and J. Raymond, *A History of the Frozen Meat Trade* (London, 1912)

Cronon, William, *Nature's Metropolis* (London, 1991)

Davis, Simon J. M., *The Archaeology of Animals* (London, 1987)

Daix, Pierre, *Picasso: Life and Art*, trans. Olivia Emmet (London, 1993)

deJohn Anderson, Virginia, *Creatures of Empire: How Domesticated Animals Transformed Early America* (Oxford, 2004)

Dobie, J. Frank, *The Longhorns* (London, 1943)

—, *Cow People* (Texas, 1964)

Evans-Pritchard, E. E., *The Nuer* (Oxford, 1974)

Ford, Brian J., *BSE: The Facts* (London, 1996)

Fraser, Alan, *The Bull* (Reading, 1972)

Frazer, J. G., *The Golden Bough: A Study in Magic and Religion*, abridged edn (reprinted London, 1987)

Galaty, J. G., and P. Bonte, eds, *Herders, Warriors and Traders: Pastoralism in Africa* (Oxford, 1991)

Galton, Francis, *The Art of Travel, 1872* (reprinted London, 1971)

Grandin, Temple, *Animals in Translation* (London, 2005)

Graves, Robert, *The Greek Myths* (London, 1992)

Greg, I. M., and S. H. Towers, *Cattle Ships and our Meat Supply* (London, 1894)

Hall, Stephen, and Juliet Clutton-Brock, *Two Hundred Years of British Farm Livestock* (London, 1989)

Harris, Marvin, *Cows, Pigs, Wars and Witches* (New York, 1989)

Hemingway, Ernest, *Death in the Afternoon,* (London, 1932)

—, *The Sun Also Rises* (New York, 1926)

Herskovits, Melville J., *The Cattle Complex in East Africa* (1927)

Houghton Brodrick, A., ed., *Animals in Archaeology* (London, 1972)

Hughes, Robert, *Goya* (London, 2003)

Kean, Hilda, *Animal Rights* (London, 1998)

Lester, Horace Francis, *Behind the Scenes in Slaughterhouses* (London, 1892)

Lewis, Jon E., *The Mammoth Book of the West* (London, 2001)

Lodrick, Deryck O., *Sacred Cows, Sacred Places* (London, 1981)

Mallet, Gina, *Last Chance To Eat: The Fate of Taste in a Fast Food World* (Edinburgh, 2005)

Marvin, Garry, *Bullfight* (Oxford, 1988)

Mourant, A. E., and F. E. Zeuner, eds, *Man and Cattle: Proceedings of a Symposium on Domestication* (Royal Anthropological Institute, 1963)

Rath, Sara, *About Cows* (Minocqua, WI, 1988)

Perren, Richard, *The Meat Trade in Britain, 1840–1914* (London, 1978)

Renault, Mary, *The King Must Die* (London, 1958)

Rice, Michael, *The Power of the Bull* (London, 1998)

Rifkin, Jeremy, *Beyond Beef: The Rise and Fall of the Cattle Culture* (London, 1992)

Ritvo, Harriet, *The Animal Estate: The English and Other Creatures in the Victorian Age* (Cambridge, MA, 1987)

Rogers, Ben, *Beef and Liberty: Roast Beef, John Bull and the English Nation* (London, 2004)

Scott, Manda, *Boudica: Dreaming The Bull* (London, 2004)

Sherratt, Andrew, 'Plough and Pastoralism: Aspects of the Secondary Products Revolution', in Ian Hodder, Glynn Isaac and Norman Hammond, eds, *Pattern of the Past: Studies in Honour of David Clarke* (Cambridge, 1981)

Schlosser, Eric, *Fast Food Nation* (London, 2001)

Shubert, Adrian, *Death and Money in the Afternoon* (Oxford, 1999)

Sinclair, Upton, *The Jungle* (New York, 1906)

Singer, Peter, *Animal Liberation*, 2nd edn (London, 1995)

Skaggs, Jimmy M., *Prime Cut: Livestock Raising and Meatpacking in the us* (College Station, TX, 1986)

Smith, Andrew B., *Pastoralism in Africa: Origins and Development Ecology* (London, 1992)

Starkey, Paul, 'The History of Working Animals in Africa', in R. M. Blench and K. MacDonald, eds, *The Origins and Development of African Livestock* (London, 2000)

Sterchi, Beat, *The Cow* (London, 1988)

Swabe, Joanna, *Animals, Disease and Human Society* (London, 1999)

Taylor, Lonn, and Ingrid Maar, *The American Cowboy* (Washington, DC, 1983)

Thomas, Keith, *Man and the Natural World: Changing Attitudes in England, 1500–1800* (London, 1983)

van Vuure, Cis, *Retracing the Aurochs* (Sofia and Moscow, 2005)

Webster, John, *Understanding the Dairy Cow* (Oxford, 1987)

Wünschmann, A., 'The Wild and Domestic Oxen', in Grzimek's *Animal Life Encyclopedia*, vol. XIII: *Mammals iv* (New York, 1972)

Associations and Websites

OKLAHOMA STATE UNIVERSITY ANIMAL SCIENCE DEPARTMENT
www.ansi.okstate.edu/breeds/cattle/
Descriptions of the cattle breeds of the world

THE BOVINE BAZAAR
www.bovinebazaar.com/breedassoc.htm
A near-complete list of global cattle breed associations

OTHER ASSOCIATIONS INCLUDE:
www.gloucestercattle.org.uk

www.irishmoiledcattlesociety.com

www.lincolnredcattlesociety.co.uk

www.longhorncattlesociety.com

SEE 'REFERENCES' FOR SUGGESTED WEBSITES, PLUS:

www.aurochs.org/cows/famous/
List of, and links to, 'famous' cows

www.crazyforcows.com
Popular website for cow enthusiasts; springboard site for many
other cow-related internet links

www.prairieoxdrovers.com
   Canadian oxen enthusiasts; many links to oxen-related websites

www.ciwf.org.uk
   Compassion in World Farming website

http://members.tripod.com/~animom/bull.html
   The Extreme Cruelty of Bullfighting – anti-bullfight website

www.iscowp.org
   The International Society for Cow Protection

Acknowledgements

I would like to acknowledge Jonathan Burt for all his encouragement and advice – without him I would not have written this book. Also thanks to Harry Gilonis for his patience. Thanks lastly to Grant Sherriffs and to my parents, Tim and Pauline: no more cow-talk, I promise.

This book is for my brother, Christian Velten, who has been missing in Africa since March 2003 after setting out to follow in the footsteps of the Scottish explorer Mungo Park. May the 'special' cows be looking after him.

Photo Acknowledgements

The author and publishers wish to express their thanks to the below sources of illustrative material and/or permission to reproduce it. (Some sources uncredited in the captions for reasons of brevity are also given below.)

Photo Seth N. Anderson: p. 92; Archaeological Museum of Herakleion: pp. 40, 50; Acropolis Museum, Athens: p. 41; Albright-Knox Art Gallery, Buffalo: p. 90; photo courtesy of the artist (Michael J. Austin) / Park Walk Gallery, London: p. 6; drawings by the author: pp. 11, 99; photo Leonardo Beraldo: p. 165; Bibliothèque Nationale de France, Paris: p. 81; British Library, London: pp. 102 (MS 4213of.170), 128 (MS Royal 2.B.VII.f.75), British Museum, London: pp. 24-25, 32, 117 (BM Orient 533); Cairo Museum: p. 71; photo Frans Devriese: p. 113; Egyptian Museum, Cairo: p. 68; photo Porter Glendinning: p. 38; photo Naveen Jamal: p. 170; Karachi Museum: p. 22; photo courtesy of John Kenny / Sparshatt Galleries, London: p. 9; photo Mark Kerrison: p. 78; Koninklijk Kabinet van Schilderijen 'Mauritshuis', Den Haag: p. 87; Kunsthistorisches Museum, Vienna: p. 83; photo Enrico Laçet: p. 18; photos Library of Congress, Washington, DC, Prints and Photographs Division: pp. 27 (British Cartoon Prints Collection, LC-USZC4-3147), 28 (LC-USZ62-100542), 33 (LC-USZC4-10065), 51 (LC-USZ62-102085), 62 (LC-USZC4-6784), 64 (LC-USZ62-91677), 69 (LC-USZ62-113356), 85 (LC-USZ62-112640), 94 (LC-USZ61-1026), 103 (photo Fred Niblo, LC-DIG-ppmsca-04931), 104 foot (photo John F. Jarvis, LC-USZ62-64854), p. 109 (LC-USZ62-72566), 121 (LC-USZ62-94687), 132 (British Cartoon Prints Collection, LC-USZ62-132986), 139

(LC-USZ62-97324), 141 (American Folklife Centre, LC-USZ62-2669), 144 (photo F. M. Steele, LC-USZ62-55219), 145 (LC-USZ62-106852), 146 (LC-USZ62-89989), 152 (Frank and Frances Carpenter Collection, LC-USZ62-99484), 173 (LC-USZ62-51759), 174 foot (LC-USZ62-51781); reproduced courtesy of the Montana Stockgrowers' Association and the Montana Historical Society: p. 150; Musée du Louvre, Paris: pp. 35, 48; Musée Eugène Boudin, Honfleur: p. 47; Museo Capitolino, Rome: p. 42; Musée d'Orsay, Paris: p. 63; Museo Nazionale, Naples: p. 29; National Gallery of Scotland, Edinburgh: p. 129 (top); National Museum, Athens: p. 49; National Museum, Copenhagen: p. 43; photo 1 2 3 oochappan: p. 54 (www.pbase.com/oochappan); Palace Museum, Beijing: p. 98; Palazzo Ducale, Venice: p. 39; photo Colin Gregory Palmer: p. 162 (www.Colin GregoryPalmer.net); photos Rex Features: p. 106 (Rex Features / Sipa Press, 203792C), 116 (Rex Features / Pacific Press Service, 94255D), 122 (Rex Features / K. Nomachi, 294915BE), 124 (Rex Features / Paul Grover, 538263M), 163 (Rex Features / Greg Williams, 260105A), 167 (Rex Features / Simon Townsley, 238999A), (Rex Features / Richard Austin, 335879E); photo Tim Robson: p. 151; Roger-Viollet: p. 174 top (3960-10, courtesy of Rex Features); photo Richard Shilling: p. 79; Solomon R. Guggenheim Museum, New York: p. 89; photo Hartmut Ulrich: p. 123; photo John Warburton-Lee photography: p. 119; photo Ellen Wallace / Zidao Communication, Switzerland: p. 74; collection of Jan Wichers, Hamburg: p. 75; photo Matthew Winterburn: p. 95.

Index